COLOUR LIBRARY OF SCIENCE
MATHEMATICS

COLOUR LIBRARY OF SCIENCE
MATHEMATICS

IRENE FEKETE & JASMINE DENYER

ORBIS · LONDON

First published in Great Britain by
Orbis Publishing Limited, London 1984

Reprinted 1986 by Orbis Book Publishing
Corporation Ltd.
A BPCC plc company

Printed in Yugoslavia
10 9 8 7 6 5 4 3 2

Mathematics
ISBN: 0-85613-767-7

Colour Library of Science
ISBN: 0-85613-585-2

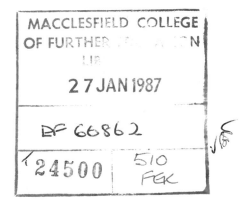
Previous pages
Operations control at
the Goddard Space
Center, Maryland,
during the launch of the
STS-6 space shuttle in
April 1983. You can see
the shuttle on the big
screen.

Editor Penny Clarke
Designer Roger Kohn

CONTENTS

▲Detail of the decoration on the walls of the Alcazar in Seville, Spain. It shows the highly complicated geometrical patterns the Arab architects used.

Note There are some unusual words in this book. They are explained in the Glossary on pages 62–63. The first time each word is used in the text it is printed in *italics*.

I WHAT MATHEMATICS IS

MATHEMATICS EVERYWHERE

► Snow crystals are perfect examples of the beautiful mathematical shapes we find everywhere in nature. No two snow crystals are ever alike but each is always symmetrical. This means that if you cut one across the middle, each half is a perfect reflection of the other.

How many languages do you know? Just one? Perhaps you are learning one or two more now. You may know a few words in several different languages: names of things to eat, songs, how to say 'please' and 'thank you' or a prayer. Families that have strong ties with other countries or cultures often speak a second language at home. If you answered the question quickly, you probably did not think of including what you know of a very special language. Everyone in the world knows at least a little of it. People need it in some way every day. No business could be done without its help. Every shop and store in the world would close at once if it did not exist. What is this universal language? Mathematics.

Mathematics uses numbers, signs, shapes and patterns instead of words. In other languages, the rules of grammar show us how to put words in the right form and the right order so we can express our ideas and link them together. Grammar is like a skeleton that holds together and gives shape to the words we use when we speak, read or write. Mathematics is just like that too. It has clear rules that show how numbers, spaces, patterns and many other things can be joined together, separated, combined and changed to describe and explain ideas.

A baby learns language step by step. A very small baby cannot use much language or explain itself easily. Often only its parents can understand it. As it grows, it learns from the world around it. Schools teach special language skills like reading and writing. Eventually the child becomes an adult who can speak easily about anything. Everyone who knows the language can understand what is being said.

Mathematics as a language

We learn mathematics in much the same way. We can see many of its basic ideas in everyday life. Pouring water into different shaped jugs teaches us something about measuring. Counting different sorts of fruit on a table introduces numbers and sets. Cutting out paper snowflakes for Christmas decorations introduces mathematical *symmetry*. At school, we learn more about these ideas and how to use them. Eventually, as our skills improve, we find we can explain difficult ideas very neatly and precisely using mathematics, not words.

People interested in *science* study mathematics until they can use it comfortably at a highly complicated level. Scientists work to understand, describe and sometimes control many things that happen in the physical world. They need a very exact language for their work. A *chemist*, for example, wants to know precisely what happens when he mixes two chemicals together. Will they do something useful or something dangerous? How much of each does he need to achieve the same results again and again? A doctor testing a new drug must know how much is safe to use. What pattern of events occurs when the drug is used on animals in the laboratory? *Physicists*, trying to understand what happens inside an *atom*, the smallest unit of matter in the universe, need mathematics to express what they discover.

People who study the applied sciences, such as engineering, also need good mathematical understanding. Mathematics helps someone design a beautiful and strong bridge or an efficient engine. In business and banking, mathematics helps people make decisions. Because mathematics is so important and useful, it is sad that too many people stop studying it at an early age. When this happens, they often find themselves stuck, like a child that has not grown up, able to understand only a few ideas and use just the basic, least interesting skills.

▼ The art and science of using numbers, arithmetic, is often the first part of mathematics we meet at school. This little girl is discovering what sort of patterns numbers can make. This sort of experience will help her understand mathematical rules and not just learn them off by heart.

◀ The atom bomb is the most spectacular proof of a mathematical law that mankind has ever seen. Albert Einstein, a very great mathematician, formulated a mathematical relationship between energy and matter. Other scientists, using his ideas, were able to split atoms and release the tremendous energy inside them.

THINKING WITH NUMBERS

	0	1	2	3	4	5	6	7	8	9	10
Babylonian		𒁹	𒈫	𒐈	𒐉	𒐊	𒐋	𒐌	𒐍	𒐎	⟨
Egyptian		I	II	III	IIII	III/II	III/III	III/III	IIII/IIII	III/III	∩
Mayan	⬭	•	••	•••	••••	—	•/—	••/—	•••/—	••••/—	=
Greek		Α	Β	Γ	Δ	Ε	F	Z	H	⊙	I
Chinese		一	二	三	四	五	六	七	八	九	十
Roman		I	II	III	IV	V	VI	VII	VIII	IX	X
Hindu	0	1	2	3	8	9	6	1	8	9	
Arabic	.	١	٢	٣	٤	٥	٦	٧	٨	٩	
modern	0	1	2	3	4	5	6	7	8	9	10

▲ Here are some ancient and modern ways of writing numbers. The Babylonians who lived centuries before the birth of Christ used wedge-shaped marks pressed into damp clay. The Mayans lived in Central America from about 1000 BC until the Spanish Conquest in the 16th century. Modern numbers replaced Roman numerals when the Europeans had a chance to study the work of Arabic mathematicians at the time of the Crusades (11th to 13th centuries).

Mathematics begins with numbers. All languages in the world have words for numbers. But what exactly is a number? A number is a symbol – such as four or 4 – that stands for a particular 'how many' or shows us precisely where something belongs in a list or sequence of things. Mathematics today uses many symbols – different marks or signs that have a special meaning – but numbers are the most ancient ones and the ones we learn first.

When ancient people began to use numbers they noticed that there is a wonderful order about them. Patterns of numbers can be repeated perfectly again and again if the same numbers are combined or separated in the same way. Numbers were more exact than ordinary words to describe the size and shape of things. *Philosophers* noticed that if they wanted to think about quantities or how things could relate to each other, numbers helped them think clearly and precisely. They also came to see that there were many different kinds of number and these could be arranged in different *systems* and used in different ways.

The numbers we know best, the series that begins 1, 2, 3, 4..., are called whole numbers. Another name for them is *integers*. Although we now write them very differently from the way they were written by the Egyptians, Greeks and Romans, each number today is used in exactly the same way as it was then. We use whole numbers in different ways but chiefly for counting. It does not matter what we want to count, large or small, alive or not. We count sheep the same way we count bricks.

We group our numbers in tens; our system is called the decimal system – the ten system – and we know it well as we count our money in it. Other people have used different groupings; the Romans grouped their numbers in fives, and the Babylonians in sixties. Computers are based on a grouping in twos, called the binary system.

Sometimes we need to think about negative quantities. We may need to describe how air can be colder than ice, for example. Mathematicians give us a way to do this too. They invented a way of writing 'nothing', by using 'zero'. Not only does zero (or nought) make it easy to deal with large numbers but it can also be used to divide all numbers into two groups, positive and negative.

Negative numbers
Negative numbers are easy to understand if you imagine all the whole numbers in the universe written in an unending line. Put zero in the middle of the line. The numbers on the right increase and are positive, the numbers on the left decrease and are negative. You will also notice that there gaps between each dot. We have all measured something and found that it is not quite, or just a little bit more than, a whole number. Mathematics has a special number system to cope with this problem too.

Rational numbers
Rational numbers are those we use to describe the relationship – the ratio – between one whole number and another whole number. An integer is one kind of rational number: some examples of integers written as ratios are:

$$\frac{4}{2} = 2; \frac{3}{1} = 3.$$

32	16	8	4	2	1	
1	0	1	1	0	0	32 + 8 + 4 = 44
0	0	0	1	0	1	4 + 1 = 5
0	0	1	0	1	1	8 + 2 + 1 = 11
1	1	1	1	1	1	32 + 16 + 8 + 4 + 2 + 1 = 63

◀ The binary system is based on twos. The value of each place is double that of the place on the right. If you do not want to count a particular column, you put a zero in it. This system is most often used by computers because each place can be marked by a simple 'on' or 'off' switch.

'Proper' fractions, such as $\frac{1}{2}$, are also rational numbers, and fit in between the whole numbers.

Irrational numbers

Mathematicians have discovered some other numbers that are not rational and cannot be expressed as the ratio between two integers. These are called irrational numbers. An example is the number which says how many times you have to multiply the diameter of a circle to find its circumference; this number starts off as 3.14159... and goes on for ever. We usually write it as π.

type of system	third place	second place	first place
base 10 system	2	0	I
base 7 system	2	0	I
base 3 system	2	0	I

base 10 system

I unit + 0 tens + 2 hundreds = I + 0 + 200 = 201

base 7 system

I unit + 0 sevens + 2 forty-nines = I + 0 + 98 = 99

base 3 system

I unit + 0 threes + 2 nines = I + 0 + 18 = 19

◀ Different number systems organize how numbers are written and what their value is in many ways so it is always important to know what the base of the system is. Here we see three different systems. In a base 3 system, the second column is 3 times the value of the first, the third 9 times the value of the first and so on. The base 10 or decimal system is the one we use most often.

Imaginary numbers

Another special number system, imaginary numbers, has been invented to deal with the problem of finding a number which, when multiplied by itself, gives a negative answer. Imaginary numbers are very useful to physicists when they try to describe such things as how energy works.

▶Ten different notes from ten different countries using ten different sorts of currency! Clockwise from the top they are: America, Germany, Spain, Sweden, Italy, Greece, Britain, Switzerland, France and the Netherlands.

WORKING WITH NUMBERS

Arithmetic introduces most of us to formal mathematics. With numbers, arithmetic uses four basic operations: addition, subtraction, multiplication and division. As we do different sorts of calculations – working out problems using numbers – we learn how to use those operations. We begin in a simple way, using small whole numbers. Then we learn how to handle larger numbers and complicated calculations that may use two or more operations to complete. We progress to fractions and decimals. Arithmetic prepares us for some of the more advanced mathematical ideas and skills we will meet in other branches of mathematics such as algebra and trigonometry.

Basic arithmetic

The basis of all arithmetic is classification: sorting things into groups of like or unlike members. From classification, we can count how many things there are in a group (enumeration); how many things in several groups are of different sizes (addition); how many things in several groups are of the same size (multiplication); we can compare different sized groups (subtraction); we can split a large group into several smaller groups

all the same size as each other (division). We discover the relationships between addition, multiplication, subtraction and division. Multiplication is a kind of fast addition; subtraction is a kind of backward addition – what must we add to a smaller number to obtain a larger one? Division is the opposite of multiplication: if 5 children have 6 sweets each, altogether they have $5 \times 6 = 30$ sweets; if you want to share a bag of 30 sweets equally between 5 children, they would each get $30 \div 5 = 6$.

▼ Multiplication is a shortened form of adding. You could find out how many blocks there are in this diagram by counting them. It is faster to notice that there are five groups of four blocks. Then, add these groups:
$4 + 4 + 4 + 4 + 4$ or
$5 + 5 + 5 + 5$. An even quicker way is to multiply 5×4 or 4×5. The multiplication table is worked out by repeatedly adding on the same number.

▼ A Scottish mathematician, John Napier (1550–1617), invented a series of rods or bones to make multiplication a series of easy additions. There is one rod for each number from zero to nine. The number is at the top and the multiples of it go down the rod. The diagram shows how to work out 137×4. Use the rods for 1, 3 and 7. Then, looking down at the fourth row, start on the left, add the number on the right of one rod to the one on the left of the next. These are $4 + 1$, $2 + 2$, and $8 + 0$. Their sums are 5, 4, and 8. So the answer of 4×137 is 548.

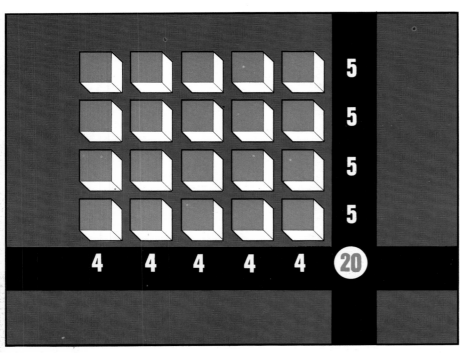

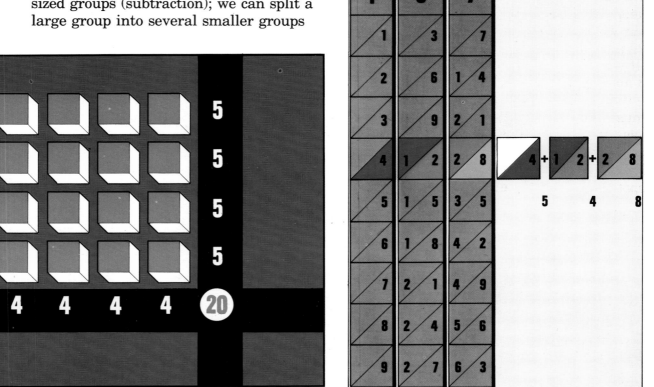

Napier's rods

$137 \times 4 = 548$

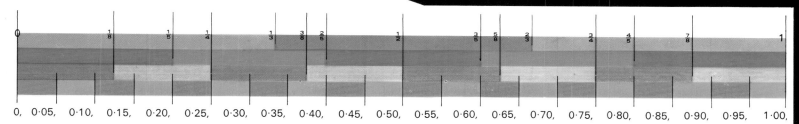

0,	0·05,	0·10,	0·15,	0·20,	0·25,	0·30,	0·35,	0·40,	0·45,	0·50,	0·55,	0·60,	0·65,	0·70,	0·75,	0·80,	0·85,	0·90,	0·95,	1·00,

In the past, primary school mathematics usually dealt only with basic arithmetic. Classes were boring. Children spent long hours practising addition, multiplication, subtraction and division – especially 'long' division, dividing one very large number by another large number. But not much time was spent on discussing how to tackle real problems which need arithmetic, so often children did not know whether they should be adding or multiplying. Nowadays we have calculators to do the slog work of 'sums', and spend a lot of time on making sure that pupils know what to do to solve a problem. A calculator is the modern aid to calculation but there have always been such aids, for example the abacus and Napier's bones.

Using calculators
Even though we use calculators, it is still very important that we know all our easy number patterns and our tables. By a 'number pattern' we mean results that keep cropping up that help us to check our work: 3 plus 7 is 10; 13 plus 7 is 20; 23 plus 47 is 70: can you see a pattern? (If you add any two numbers that end in 3 and 7 your answer will always end in 0 – if it is correct!) For the same reason we must know the multiplication tables; it is easy to make a small mistake on a calculator and enter a wrong number, but knowing the tables makes it easier to spot the error when checking the answer.

When we use calculators we must always ask ourselves at the end if our answer makes sense. A *calculator display* of our answer may show a lot of noughts after the other figures, and we must know if our answer is to be in the tens, or hundreds, or thousands. Suppose you want to know how long it will take you to drive 126 miles at an average speed of 42 miles an hour: your calculator may show the answer as 30000000 – how many of those noughts do you need? Do you need any? Before putting the sum on the calculator, ask yourself 'Are there some easier numbers that are near to the ones I have to use? Suppose the problem was 120 miles at 40 miles an hour: how many 40s in 120? 3. So the answer to the problem is going to be something like 3, and not 30 or 300.'

It is a very good habit to look around you and try to 'estimate' or make a sensible guess at the size of things around you; how tall is the cherry tree in your garden? If you cannot guess, reason it out: is it taller than a man? How many men standing on each others' shoulders would reach the top? Probably two, and then a little bit more. How tall is a man? A bit less than 1.8 m (6 ft). So two men and a bit make about 3.5 m to 4 m (12 ft or 13 ft), which gives you a good idea of the height of your cherry tree.

You can have a lot of fun setting yourself problems like this, and at the same time it will help you use your calculator sensibly.

▲ This chart compares two different sorts of fraction and the way they are expressed in numbers. The top line shows ordinary fractions where a unit – one item – has been divided into halves, thirds, quarters, fifths, eighths, and tenths. The bottom line shows how the same unit can be divided into decimal fractions, tenths, and how each fraction would be written in the decimal system.

▼ A Japanese business man is using an abacus, a frame with movable beads that helps him do calculations quickly. Somone who is very skilled with an abacus can add, subtract, multiply and divide almost as rapidly as a machine. The abacus was first developed by the Romans, then adopted by the Chinese and Japanese who still use it today.

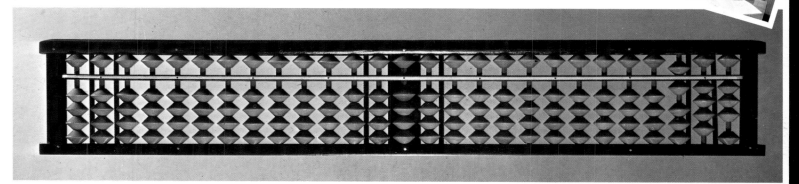

WORKING WITH SYMBOLS

Algebra takes us farther into the world of mathematical thought. It uses numbers but has other symbols as well, chiefly letters of the alphabet, especially x. The symbols make it possible for us to investigate unknown numbers or quantities. If you tell someone you need five apples to make a pudding and are going to buy two more but do not say how many you already have, you could not write that down in arithmetic. In algebra you can, by saying $x + 2 = 5$. The x stands for the unknown number of apples you already have. In more complicated problems with several unknowns, other letters of the alphabet are used.

More varied and complicated problems can be set out clearly in algebra because it has a richer symbolic language than arithmetic. The familiar plus and minus signs are used for addition and subtraction but multiplication and division are indicated differently. To show that two numbers are to be multiplied we place them side by side with no symbol between them. For example $3a$ means 3 times whatever number a stands for. Also xy means that the number y stands for is multiplied by the number x represents. If we need to say that a number must be multiplied by itself several times, this is easily done by using a small number put slightly above and to the right of the main number, x^2. The small number is called an exponent. x^2 thus means x times x. Division is indicated by fractions.

When we see $\frac{x}{3}$ it means that whatever x stands for is divided by 3.

When we want to compare things, algebra has special symbols to show whether one thing is the same size, larger than, or smaller than, another. The first symbol we recognize from arithmetic, = which means 'equals'. The other two are > which means 'is larger than' and < which means 'is smaller than'.

Equations

Equations are statements in algebra where the total value on the left of the equal sign must be exactly the same as that on the right. An inequality is

▲ Europeans learned many of the rules of algebra from the Arabs in the 14th century. The word algebra itself comes from the title of an arabic book on mathematics and it means 'joining together'.

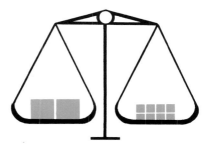

◄ The two sides of an equation are like two pans on an old-fashioned scale. Each side must balance the other perfectly. Whatever change you make to one side you must make to the other. Here we see how to discover the value of x by subtraction and division. $2x + 3 = 11$. By subtracting 3 from each side you can see that $2x$ balances 8 and the equation is made more simple. Finally, by dividing each side in half, you discover $x = 4$.

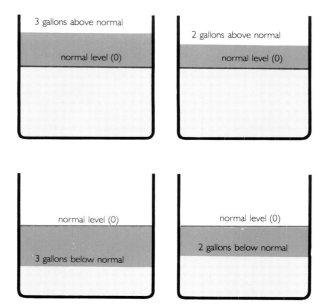

◄ Algebra uses positive and negative numbers so sometimes the plus and minus signs are used to mean this instead of addition or subtraction. Positive numbers are used in this drawing to show the amount of water in a tank above its normal or usual level. Negative numbers show how much less than normal is there. Zero is used for the normal level. Note that $+3$ is more water than $+2$ but -3 represents less water than -2.

another kind of algebraic statement. It can be true for many values of an unknown number whereas an equation is true only for certain values. When people talk about solving equations, they mean they work out what the unknowns stand for. Some equations can have several correct solutions. This makes them very different from ordinary calculations in arithmetic.

Algebra is particularly helpful in problem solving. First you put together an equation that correctly describes the problem. Sometimes just one equation will not be enough and several are needed. These are called simultaneous equations and they can often be worked out using a graph. To be able to solve equations where there are several unknown quantities, there must be as many equations as there are unknowns. If there are four unknown quantities, you must have four equations; otherwise you will not be able to find values for all the unknowns.

▼The equation $x + 2y = 10$ has many solutions. These are three of them. Can you find some more values for x and y that satisfy the equation?

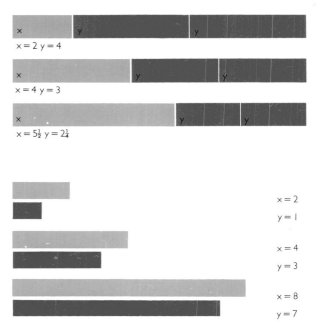

$x = 2\ y = 4$

$x = 4\ y = 3$

$x = 5\frac{1}{2}\ y = 2\frac{1}{4}$

$x = 2$
$y = 1$

$x = 4$
$y = 3$

$x = 8$
$y = 7$

◄ There are so many answers to the equation $x - y = 1$ that we could never count them all; here we see three correct but different values for each symbol.

BEAUTIFUL AND USEFUL

If arithmetic and algebra provide the hard-working grammar of mathematics, geometry – for all its usefulness – adds a dash of art and philosophy. Geometry describes, compares and makes it possible for us to measure all the different shapes we see around us. Stop and think for a moment just how many there are. Some are flat with edges. Some are round. Some are thick and can be filled with other things of different shapes or something that can alter its shape, like

water. Even living things like plants and animals have shapes that can be described geometrically.

Being able to measure shapes is very important. Everyone needs to do it in some way at some time or other. Farmers and builders need to know how much land there is in a field to judge if they have enough for what they want to do. Anyone with a house needs to know how to work out how much carpeting to buy, how much paint will cover a wall or how many tiles will cover the bathroom floor. Even the manager of a supermarket will be helped by geometry because its rules will reveal how many and what sort of packages and containers will stack together for an attractive display and not fall down. Nearly two thousand years before Columbus set off on his famous voyage to prove the world was round, Greek mathematicians using their knowledge of geometry had worked out that the world was a sphere – shaped like an orange.

► These polygons are very familiar to look at, even if you do not know their names. We see them in many patterns on the surface of everyday things.

▼ The solid shape of the small box is built up from six squares. It is called a cube. Cubes are used to measure volume – that is how much space a solid shape takes up. Cubic measurement can be done in inches or centimeters. Using the small cube as one unit, we can see that the volume of the large cube is eight times that of the small cube.

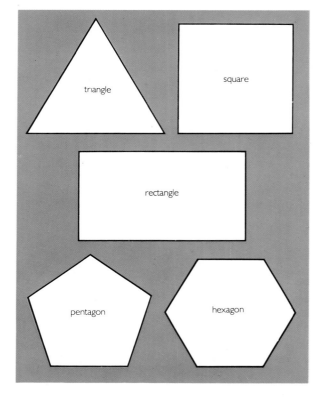

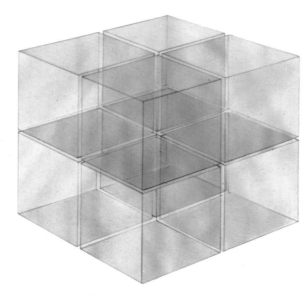

Flat shapes

Like arithmetic, geometry uses 'classification', sorting shapes into different groups by seeing what properties they have in common, and where they differ. One classification is of all those shapes that are flat, have straight sides and sharp corners. We call this group 'polygons'. (This word comes from the Greek word *poly* for 'many', and another Greek word *gonia* for 'angle'. Can you think of other 'poly-' words? Look in a dictionary to see how many there are.)

We can then divide the group of 'polygons' into smaller groups: all the three-sided ones are called triangles, those with four sides are called quadrilaterals. We can then divide the smaller groups into still smaller groups; triangles with all the sides the same length are called 'equilateral' triangles; quadrilaterals with all sides equal and all

► Human beings like geometric patterns. A satellite photograph of the Imperial Valley in California shows the regular rectangular pattern of the fields and crops.

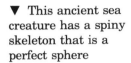

▶ Living things often grow into geometrical shapes and can be described mathematically. The snail shell grows in a curling spiral that can be described by a regular series of numbers.

▼ This ancient sea creature has a spiny skeleton that is a perfect sphere

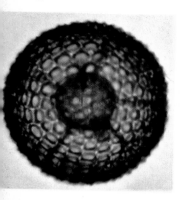

the angles 'square' (or 'right' angles) are called squares.

Sorting shapes in this way shows us that all triangles and all squares are polygons, as they all belonged to the first sorting, or first classification. But the reverse is not true: not all polygons are triangles. So we have to be careful.

Solid shapes

Another classification is of solid shapes where all the sides are polygons. These solids are called 'polyhedra' (another poly-word). You know the cube, which has six sides, each of which is a square. Do you know the tetrahedron, which has four sides, each of which is a triangle? Some cartons of milk, or of fruit juice, are made in this shape, as it is very difficult to tip over, and several of them can stack together with no spaces in between. Another classification is those shapes we get if we rotate a flat shape about its axis; a circle will rotate into a sphere; a square will rotate into a cylinder; a triangle will rotate into a cone.

In geometry we study the relationships between the different elements that make up shapes – the sides and angles of polygons, the area covered by a flat surface, the volume of a solid.

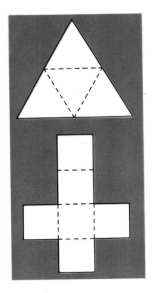

◀ Trace and cut out these two shapes. Fold along the dotted lines. The top shape makes a tetrahedron. One other shape can also be folded into a tetrahedron. Which is it? The bottom shape folds up into a cube. Can you work out the five possible shapes, or nets, that will fold up to make a cube?

Angles and degrees

An important element in many shapes is the corners. To study corners we look at how much the line along one side of the corner has to turn or rotate about the corner so that it lies along the other line. We call this amount of turning an 'angle'. Stand on one spot and hold an arm out in front of you to point at something directly ahead. Now turn right round, in a full circle, so you are again pointing at that same object. To measure an amount of turning, first think of the full circle you have just turned. Now imagine that instead of doing it in a smooth turn all at once, you had done it in a series of tiny jerks, 360 in all, all the same size. Each of these tiny jerky turns is called a 'degree'. A turn of a full circle is made up of 360 part turns, each of one degree. A turn of half a circle, so you are facing in the opposite direction to your original position, is made up of half of 360 degrees, that is, 180 degrees; a quarter turn, say from facing north to facing east, is made up of a quarter of 360 degrees, that is, 90 degrees. If you stand straight with both arms pointing ahead of you, and then turn one arm so that it is pointing out to your side, that arm has made a turn of 90 degrees, and there is a 'square' angle between your arms. The symbol ° denotes 'degree', and we write, for example, 90° or 180°. An angle of less than 90° is called an 'acute' angle, one between 90° and 180° is called 'obtuse' and one between 180° and 360° is called reflex.

Geometry and philosophy

Studying geometry has been an important part of training people to think clearly for thousands of years. One Greek philosopher had such a high opinion of the value of geometry that he remarked 'God himself is always doing geometry'. He had been deeply impressed by the vast number of perfect geometric shapes and patterns he observed in nature. Geometry as the Greeks developed it was a deductive science. All the statements it made were proved step by step from a small number of clear and undisputed 'first principles', or 'axioms'– though some of these have now been disputed.

SYMMETRY

Many of the shapes, flat and solid, studied in geometry are symmetrical. This means that a line or cut through them can divide them into two equal parts. The cutting line, or it may be the folding line if the shape is made of cloth or paper, is called the axis of symmetry. Some shapes have more than one axis, a square has four. Two cut the square into matching rectangles, two others divide it into equal triangles. A triangle whose sides are all exactly the same length or equal is called an equilateral triangle. It has three axes of symmetry (axes is the plural of axis). A circle, one of the most fascinating shapes, has an infinite number. This means you can draw an

unlimited number of axes through its centre and still have equal halves.

Shapes that cannot be divided symmetrically are called asymmetric. But it is possible to make new symmetric shapes with them. Draw a triangle with each side a different length. Look at its reflection in a mirror. Although it has the same sides and angles, it looks different because it is back to front. Cut out the asymmetric triangle. Draw its reflection and cut it out. Put the triangles down side by side with two sides of equal length touching. That becomes an axis of symmetry. The new shape may have either three or four sides. If you do the experiment with a solid shape made out

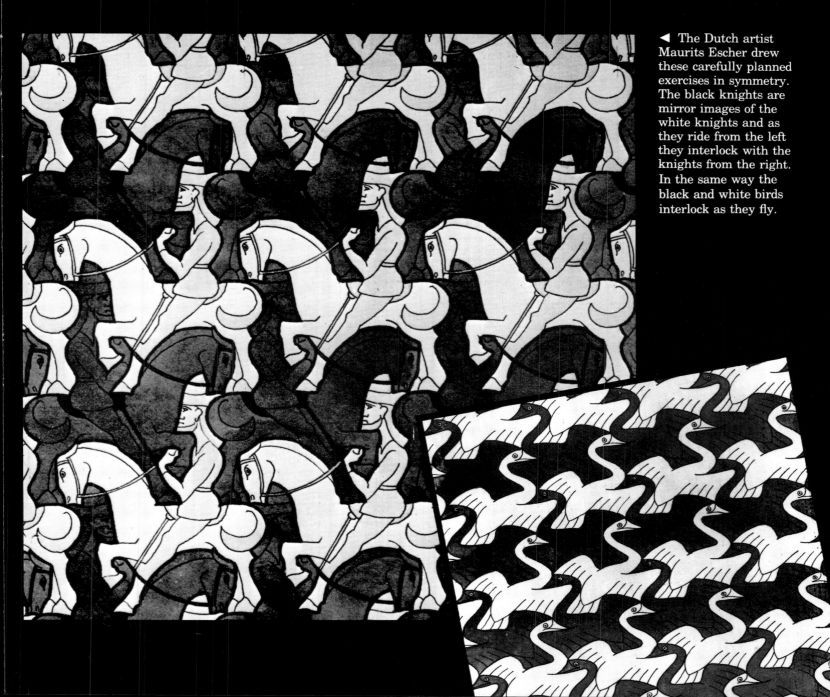

◀ The Dutch artist Maurits Escher drew these carefully planned exercises in symmetry. The black knights are mirror images of the white knights and as they ride from the left they interlock with the knights from the right. In the same way the black and white birds interlock as they fly.

► The molecules of this crystal have surfaces that are isosceles triangles. That means two sides of the triangle match but the base is different. They fasten together symmetrically until they 'grow' into the pyramid shape we see here.

▼ The toy windmill on the left and its mirror image on the right show rotational symmetry. Each blade is at the same angle and the blades form the same pattern as they turn. Neither real windmill nor its image are bilaterally symmetrical.

b

of clay or plasticine, the joining point is the *plane* of symmetry.

The parts of a symmetrical shape or object are not just equal and balanced, they are mirror-images of each other. Our bodies are more or less symmetrical. You can understand the mirror image idea if you try to put your left hand on top of your right with both palms down. They won't match. Put your palms together and they will. All two-sided symmetry is called bilateral.

Rotational symmetry
Another kind of symmetry is called rotational. It describes a shape that is unchanged in appearance when it is turned or rotated by a certain amount. A good example is the propeller of a small airplane, where three blades come from the central knob and the angle between each blade is 120°. When the propeller turns 120°, each blade moves into the position another has left so it looks exactly as it did before it began to move. Some shapes, like equilateral triangles, have both bilateral and rotational symmetry.

Practical symmetry
Symmetry is far more than a beautiful or curious geometric fact. Even the smallest clusters of matter, *molecules*, have different kinds of symmetry, and this affects the way they group together. Molecules of frozen water join together symmetrically to form snow flakes. Molecules of different sorts of chemicals join on their planes of symmetry to make useful crystals. In people, symmetry is often the basis for physical beauty. Often, when we say someone is beautiful, what we really mean is that their features and body have a perfect symmetry.

▲ Our bodies have a vertical axis of symmetry running down from the middle of our heads but it is surprising how asymmetrical each side can be. With some people it is more noticable than others. These pictures show people in (a) a normal photograph (b) with the left side of the face joined to its mirror image (c) with the right side joined. Doing this to the man seems to give us three very different people. The woman has a very symmetrical face so the changes are slight.

21

WORKING WITH TRIANGLES

▶ A naval officer is calculating how far his ship must sail by using trigonometry. The curved instrument near his right hand is a protractor. It is used to measure angles.

How can you find out how tall a tree is without climbing to the top and letting down a measuring tape? How can you discover where you are in the middle of the ocean by looking at the sun? How can you calculate the height of a wall and the length of a ladder propped against it? The answer to these and many other questions, including how to aim a moon rocket, begins by saying: Use a triangle. It must be a 'right' triangle, that is one that has an angle of 90° at one of its points. The information it can provide will help you work out your problem quickly, using arithmetic and algebra as needed.

Triangles have many interesting properties; from the lengths of their sides and the size of their angles you can deduce other properties such as their area, or the size of the circle that goes through all of their points. Trigonometry, the study of triangles, has become a major branch of mathematics. In trigonometry you start by examining the relationships between the angles of a triangle, and the lengths of its sides. Trigonometry was developed during the times when sailors were exploring the world, crossing the Atlantic, sailing around Africa to India and China, sailing right around the world. They needed accurate ways of navigating, and finding where they were in the middle of vast oceans.

In tackling any mathematical problem, one of the first things to ask yourself is

'What do I know already? Can I use that to help me solve my problem?' Sailors realized that one of the things they could always know, or find out, at sea, was the angle which a pointer aimed at the sun made with the vertical. Trigonometry was the series of mathematical techniques they worked out so that this angle made by the sun would help them find their exact position.

They started by thinking about right-angled triangles, that is, triangles where one angle is 90°. They chose this because the angle between the horizontal and the vertical is 90°. Suppose you have a right-angled triangle like this:

B represents the position of the sun, the line BC represents the vertical, and the line AC the horizontal. The geometry of the Greeks helped the sailors to realize that the ratios between pairs of sides would always be the same, so long as the angles of the triangle did not change; a triangle with longer sides but the same angles would give the same ratios. They gave names to these ratios: tangent, sine and cosine, usually written as tan, sin and cos. In our triangle above:

BC divided by AC $\left(\dfrac{BC}{AC}\right)$ is called tan(gent) A

BC divided by AB $\left(\dfrac{BC}{AB}\right)$ is called sin(e) A

AC divided by AB $\left(\dfrac{AC}{AB}\right)$ is called cos(ine) A

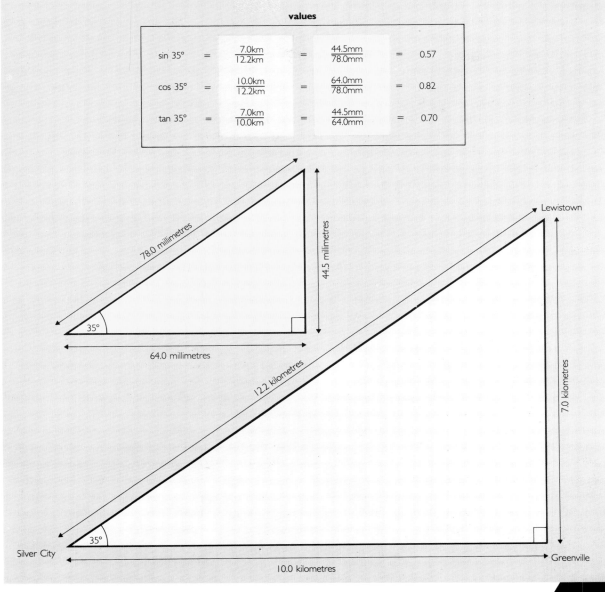

values

sin 35°	=	$\dfrac{7.0\text{km}}{12.2\text{km}}$	=	$\dfrac{44.5\text{mm}}{78.0\text{mm}}$	=	0.57
cos 35°	=	$\dfrac{10.0\text{km}}{12.2\text{km}}$	=	$\dfrac{64.0\text{mm}}{78.0\text{mm}}$	=	0.82
tan 35°	=	$\dfrac{7.0\text{km}}{10.0\text{km}}$	=	$\dfrac{44.5\text{mm}}{64.0\text{mm}}$	=	0.70

78.0 millimetres

44.5 millimetres

35°

64.0 millimetres

Lewistown

12.2 kilometres

7.0 kilometres

Silver City

35°

Greenville

10.0 kilometres

◄ These two triangles are very different in size: one is just a few millimeters and the other represents many kilometers between three towns. Although the physical measurements are so different the values for sin, cos and tan are the same.

Trigonometric tables show the values of tan, cos and sin for all possible angles (and calculators are now programmed with these values). Sailors first used a sextant to find out the angle of the sun at midday; they had also to know the date, because the sun's angle varies with the time of year and the the time of day. Then, using trigonometric tables, they could work out their exact position. They had to be sure to take the measurements exactly at midday if the tables were to be used, and this meant that they had to have very exact clocks. That is why, during the great period of world exploration in the 15th and 16th centuries, practical scientists spent a lot

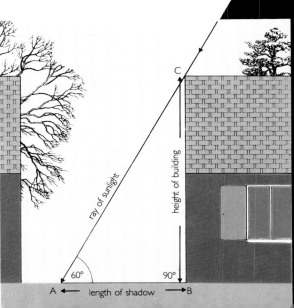

ray of sunlight

height of building

C

60°

90°

A ◄ length of shadow ► B

◄ This is how trigonometry can be used to measure the height of a house. One side, its shadow and a ray of light make up an imaginary triangle labeled A B C. The length of the shadow and the angle at which the sunlight meets it can be measured. The side BC/AB is equal to the tan(gent) of the angle of 60°. Trigonometry tables give its value as 1.732. The height of the house is tan multiplied by the length of the shadow.

2

MATHEMATICS ANCIENT AND MODERN

EARLY MATHEMATICIANS

A quick look at arithmetic, algebra, geometry and trigonometry raises more questions than it answers. Where do all these ideas and rules come from? How were they discovered? Can they change? Why is it so necessary that scientists, no matter what they are investigating, have a good knowledge of maths? How important are computers? We also may find ourselves wondering where some of the mathematical terms we have heard or learned fit in: *hypotenuse*, *set theory*, *topology*, axioms, logarithms, square roots.

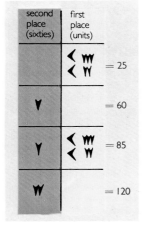

◀ The Babylonians used two wedge shaped marks to record their number system. One pointed down and represented one unit and the other pointed left and meant ten. The base of their system was 60 so in each column a symbol had 60 times the value it had in the column to its right. Both symbols could be used in each column.

second place (sixties)	first place (units)	
	◀ ₩₩ ◀ ₦	= 25
∀		= 60
∀	◀ ₩₩ ◀ ₩₩	= 85
₩₩		= 120

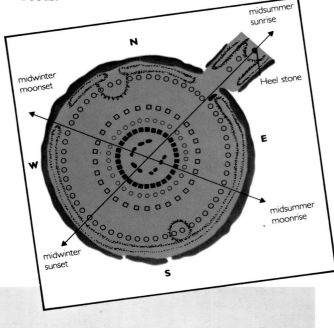

◀ Other ancient peoples used mathematically regular patterns to predict the position of the sun and moon. Stonehenge, a huge circle of standing stones on Salisbury Plain in south-west England was built about 1500 BC. It was a kind of calendar. The position of the sun or moon over certain stones set the date for important religious celebrations.

Diagram labels: N, midsummer sunrise, Heel stone, midwinter moonset, E, W, midsummer moonrise, midwinter sunset, S

The different languages people speak today have been growing and gradually changing over thousands of years. Old words are forgotten, new ones borrowed or invented. Some languages become important while the people who speak them are powerful, so their vocabulary has a great influence on others. But the basic grammar of individual languages remains remarkably constant. Mathematics is like this too. Some of the problems a modern mathematician works on would baffle one from the past. Others would be as familiar to an ancient Greek as to an astronaut. It is not just that today's student can do calculations by machine instead of spending hours, weeks, months or even years working them out by hand. Over the centuries, mathematicians and other scientists, particularly physicists and *astronomers*, have been enlarging, correcting and improving mathematical understanding and techniques.

Astronomy, studying the stars scientifically, is a link between ancient and modern mathematics. Astronomers today set up enormously complex

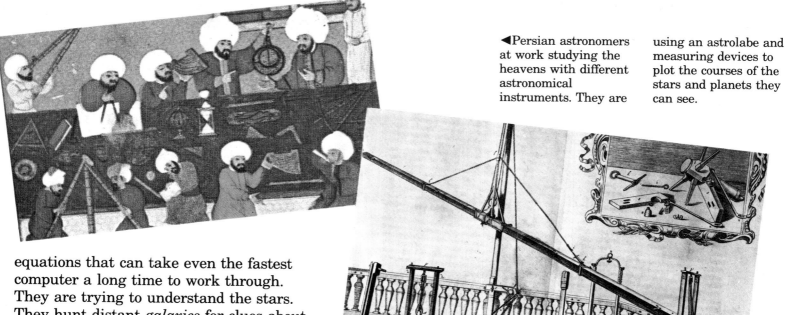

◄Persian astronomers at work studying the heavens with different astronomical instruments. They are using an astrolabe and measuring devices to plot the courses of the stars and planets they can see.

equations that can take even the fastest computer a long time to work through. They are trying to understand the stars. They hunt distant *galaxies* for clues about how the universe began or how it is likely to end. For them, mathematics is an 'applied' science, one they use constantly for practical problem solving.

Others study mathematical ideas only, some part of the *theory* that explains why numbers work the way they do when they are multiplied, for example. They investigate unusual facts that have never been fully explained, trying to make ideas clearer and more precise. For them, mathematics is a 'pure' science, studied for its own sake. It is a kind of mountain climbing of the mind. It challenges all their creative thinking skills. They are not interested in solving any immediate practical problem. Often, however, their work provides a spark of inspiration, a new way of looking at basic rules that helps applied mathematicians make progress in other fields.

Astronomy and mathematics

Four thousand years ago, in the land which is modern Iraq, people studied the stars intently. They believed that the planets were powerful gods and goddesses who influenced their lives. It was important to keep an exact record of their movement across the sky. Their observations and the records they kept by making marks on damp clay tablets was the first step towards making numbers a powerful scientific language. They noticed the orderly and regular way the stars appeared was like the orderly way numbers worked. They discovered that numerical calculations made it possible to

predict where the moon and planets would appear in the sky in the future based on where they had been in the past. Thus, using systematic observations, deductions and calculations, the ancient Babylonians and Chaldeans became the first astronomers and mathematicians in the world.

The Chinese were other very early astronomers; records of their observations help us work out when Jesus of Nazareth was born, as they recorded a very bright new star which was almost certainly the star followed by the three kings.

▲The telescope was discovered in the 17th century and astronomers soon realized how useful it was for studying the heavens. From early experimental telescopes like this have come the huge ones in our modern observatories.

◄This astronomer is not looking at the sky at all! Instead, he is checking the complex machinery which controls the enormously powerful telescope above him.

THE NEED TO MEASURE

▶ An ancient Egyptian jeweller is measuring the mass or weight of an object on a scale. Similar scales are used today. The object to be weighed is placed in one pan and standard weights in the other. When the two pans balance, the exact weight is known.

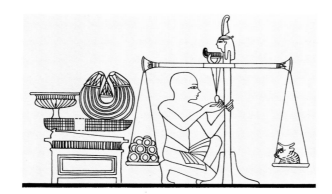

People have always asked questions like how big is it... how long... how heavy... how hot or cold... how far away? In everyday life we all need to measure things. We compare them against some unit that is always the same and then do our calculations in reference to this unit. We are most interested in measurements for length, time and mass. Mass is the bulk of something, such as the amount of flour it takes to make a loaf of bread. Providing agreed units and ways of measuring them is always an important task for mathematics. The need to do this, especially in ancient Egypt, really encouraged people to think mathematically.

▶ The first simple measurements for length or distance were based on parts of the body. The Egyptians' most important basic measurement was the cubit, the length of a man's forearm – from his elbow to the top of his middle finger. Obviously people's arms were slightly different in length so this rough and ready system gradually changed into a standard one where the units were recorded and the same one used all the time.

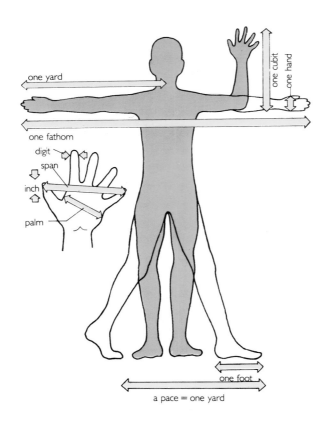

one yard

one cubit
one hand

one fathom

digit

span

inch

palm

one foot

a pace = one yard

Mathematics in ancient Egypt

All the traders who sailed the Mediterranean four thousand years ago had to use numbers in some way to keep records of how much oil, wine or wheat they sold or what was the value of their ship's cargo. The Egyptian traders did this too, but their country had more complicated measuring problems to deal with. Finding solutions to them led the Egyptians to discover the basic rules for arithmetic. They also learned how to set out simple equations. Most important of all, they deduced some of the basic principles of geometry, long before the Greeks.

Every year, the great River Nile floods vast areas of Egypt. The waters bring rich soil as well as moisture to make the valley fertile. But landmarks are washed away and the boundaries of fields shift and change. The Egyptians had a very organized way of life so they wanted to keep careful records of who owned what. Taxes paid to their king, the pharoah, were collected on the basis of how much land a man owned, so it had to be measured very precisely.

The Egyptians had reasons to be exact about other kinds of measurement as well. They built huge temples to their gods and great tombs for the pharaohs. All these holy buildings had to stand in such a way that the sun and moon passed over them in a particular way. They also had many religious festivals during the years so they needed an accurate calendar as well.

One thousand years before the birth of Christ, Ahmes, an Egyptian scribe, wrote what he called 'Directions for knowing all dark things'. He claimed to be copying and improving information gathered a thousand years earlier. What he wrote is a kind of early mathematics text book. He explained how to do addition, subtraction, multiplication and division. He paid special attention to fractions because the Egyptians found them difficult to use. He shows how to use simple numerical equations and introduces the idea of algebraic symbols. He uses the word 'heap' the way we would use *x*. The second half of his book deals largely with the sort of geometric problems the Egyptians would have to solve to measure land or build the *pyramids*.

What Ahmes wrote, and the way he wrote it, shows that even at such an early period people were fascinated by numbers and thought that knowing about them gave them power. They wanted to discover more about the way patterns and shapes could be transformed and how ideas could be clarified by being expressed in this different way.

▼The Great Pyramid at Giza in Egypt was built 4600 years ago, which shows how much the Egyptians knew about architecture.

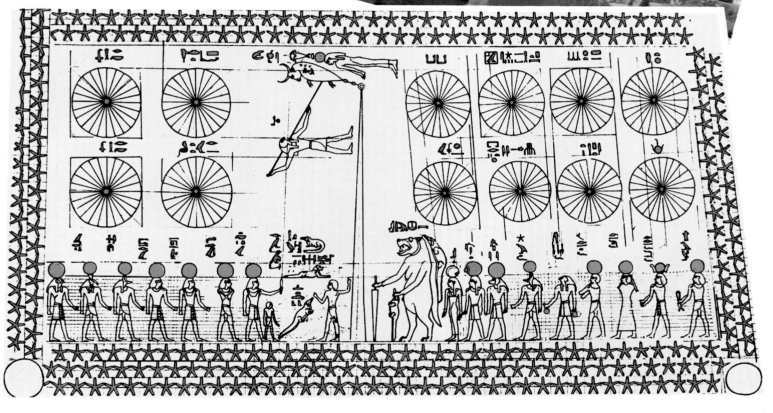

▲ An ancient Egyptian calendar. The 12 months are shown as discs. The year began on the day the Nile flooded its banks. The four discs on the left represent the season of flooding, the next four the season of sowing and the last four the harvest.

▼ These rulers, made of a hard black stone called basalt, were used by the Egyptians about 1500 BC. They record the standard cubit of the time. The Egyptians had some variations in cubit length throughout their long history. There were two kinds of cubit, an 'everyday' cubit that was about 45 cm (18 in) long and a 'royal' cubit of almost 53 cm (21 in).

THE GREEK CONNECTION

Egyptians took the first steps beyond simple arithmetic, but the Greeks established mathematics as a pure science. From the time Thales of Miletus set up the first school of philosophy and mathematics (around 600 BC) until the Romans conquered Greece (30 BC) that extraordinary country – made up of small city states, islands and colonies scattered from the shores of the Black Sea in Asia Minor to southern Italy and France – produced a string of mathematical geniuses whose work is still known and admired today.

Pythagoras and his school

Pythagoras, from the island of Samos, is one of the most famous. He travelled and studied in Egypt before setting up his school in a Greek colony in southern Italy. He believed that to study the secrets of number and shape was almost a kind of religion. You had to prepare yourself for study by living very simply and practising purity and temperance in everything you did. His classes became enormously popular and he soon had a group of disciples who called themselves Pythagoreans. They preserved and wrote down the teaching of their master because he wrote nothing himself. He taught the theory of numbers and investigated their special qualities. He applied number theory to music. He looked at what he called 'numbers at rest' – geometry, and 'numbers in motion' – astronomy. What he taught about geometry was passed on and eventually became the basis for the first two books on the subject by another famous mathematician, Euclid of Alexandria.

Because the Greeks felt that mathematics was the best training the mind could have and was the basis of all other learning, schools sprang up everywhere. Often they specialized in investigating specific ideas. For example, the Eleatic School, established in southern Italy early in the 5th century BC, looked at questions about the relationship between space, time and number. In Thrace, mathematicians

▼Pythagoras has rightly been called one of the founding fathers of the science of mathematics.

▶ Pythagoras's most famous rule or theorem is what he discovered about right angled triangles. The length of the hypotenuse squared (multiplied by itself) is equal to the squared lengths of the other two sides added together. The same will be true for any similar area drawn in proportion to the lengths of the sides.

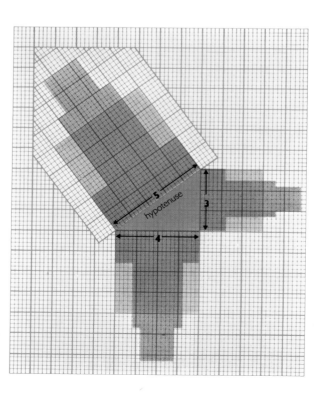

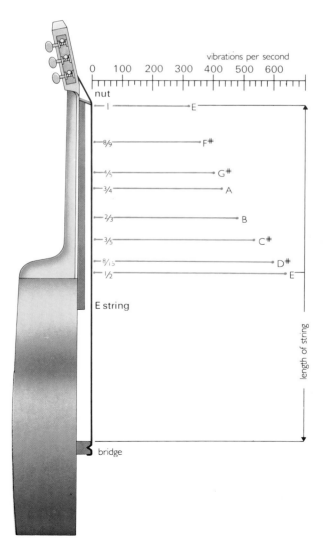

worked out the idea of the atom. Because they had no high powered microscopes or scientific equipment they could not understand atoms and molecules as we do. Using mathematics alone, however, they worked out that all *matter* was probably made out of many identical and invisible building blocks. The powerful city-state of Athens soon had an important school too. There, letters were first used to mark off sections of geometric drawings and a method was discovered so that one geometric theorem could be linked as proof to another. Aristotle, one of the school's great teachers, is better known as a philosopher than a mathematician, but he wrote important books on mathematics and mathematical physics.

The first university

His most famous pupil was not a philosopher or mathematician but a military genius. Alexander the Great conquered most of the then known world before he died at the age of 33. After his conquest of Egypt, he founded a great city near the mouth of the Nile, Alexandria. There he set up the world's first *university*. It had lecture rooms, libraries, museums, laboratories and gardens. There mathematics was studied as a subject distinct from philosophy. Teachers laid down the lines it would follow for more than a thousand years. One of its teachers, Euclid, wrote the text book on geometry that introduced millions of children to the subject through the centuries. Another great teacher of mathematics at Alexandria, Archimedes, produced a stream of wonderful inventions. He taught mathematics as a pure science but his other work made him a living link between pure and applied mathematics.

▲ Euclid, another famous mathematician, developed Pythagoras's work in geometry.

▲ Archimedes, like Euclid, taught mathematics at the university of Alexandria in Egypt.

Sieve of Eratosthenes									
	2	3	4	5	6	7	8	9	10
11	12	13	14	15	16	17	18	19	20
21	22	23	24	25	26	27	28	29	30
31	32	33	34	35	36	37	38	39	40
41	42	43	44	45	46	47	48	49	50
51	52	53	54	55	56	57	58	59	60
61	62	63	64	65	66	67	68	69	70
71	72	73	74	75	76	77	78	79	80
81	82	83	84	85	86	87	88	89	90
91	92	93	94	95	96	97	98	99	100

◀ Pythagoras observed that there were number patterns that explained how musical notes worked. When a string is shortened – by pressing it half way down its length – it vibrates twice as fast and the sound it makes is twice as high. The progression – that is the step by step movement – of sounds going up or down a scale is directly related to the vibrations of the string and its length.

▲ Eratosthenes, a mathematician who was also the librarian of the school of Alexandria for a time, invented a table to help find prime numbers. A prime number can be divided exactly only by one and itself. To find all the prime numbers up to a certain number, cross out all the multiples of two except two itself. Then cross out all the multiples of three except three itself. Continue this way for four, five and six and so on until you reach your number. The numbers left are the prime numbers.

MATHEMATICS AS MAGIC

Like other sciences, mathematical knowledge did not, and still does not, make steady progress. After the great discoveries of the Greeks it remained unchanged for centuries. For a time, it even seemed that people would lose the valuable work that had been done in the past. Remember that before AD 1500 books were rare and valuable. The Greek mathematicians originally recorded their work on thin rolls of papyrus, a kind of coarse paper made from Egyptian reeds. Roman copies were made the same way or later written on vellum, a fine calfskin. Duplicate copies of even major works were few.

When the Romans conquered Egypt, the great library of Alexandria, a treasure house of mathematical and other works, was destroyed in the fighting. Later, when the Roman Empire was overrun by barbarians, more books were lost as libraries and schools were burned

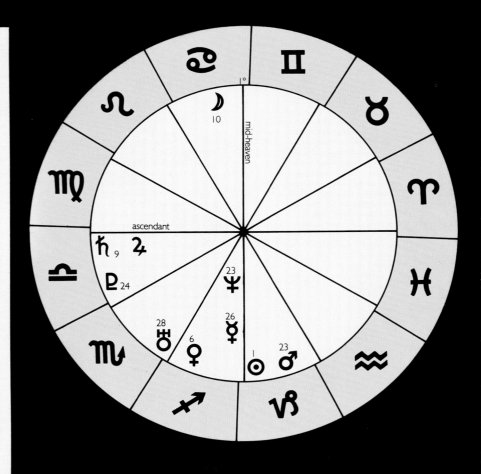

▲ The German artist, Albrecht Durer (1471–1528), was a leader of the Renaissance in Germany but he was still caught up in the tradition of thinking of mathematics as magic. Here is a magic box he designed and put in one of his paintings. Each side and diagonal adds up to 34 and so do other squares within it.

►The study of mathematics declined after the destruction of Rome in the 5th century AD. For many centuries after this people were more interested in mathematics as a form of magic, linking it with astrology in an attempt to tell the future from the movement of the planets. They also believed that they could tell a person's character by using a chart of the zodiac and marking on it the position of the different planets at the time the person was born.

♑	Capricorn
♒	Aquarius
♓	Pisces
♈	Aries
♉	Taurus
♊	Gemini
♋	Cancer
♌	Leo
♍	Virgo
♎	Libra
♏	Scorpio
♐	Sagittarius
☉	Sun
☽	Moon
☿	Mercury
♀	Venus
⊕	Earth
♂	Mars
♃	Jupiter
♄	Saturn
♅	Uranus
♆	Neptune
♇	Pluto

and teachers killed. In Europe, from around AD 500 to 1400, mathematics made little progress. No longer was it considered the best subject to train the mind. The standard of mathematics taught in the medieval universities was very poor compared to the great days in Athens and Alexandria.

In fact, doing mathematics often became little more than working out different kinds of magic spells. The ancient Greeks had understood that numbers had power. The Pythagoreans believed that everything in the world was related to number, an idea that would not seem strange to a modern scientist. But in the Middle Ages people were not as keen on discovering real mathematical facts as on finding magic numbers, perhaps in the Bible, or numbers that would work as charms. Even distinguished scholars would try to invent 'magic boxes'. In a magic box, integers are laid out in squares so that each row or column adds up to the same number. These boxes then could be engraved on gems or small squares of silver and gold and worn as charms. People believed that the numbers would frighten off devils or diseases. Some scholars taught that certain numbers 'belonged' to certain planets. They muddled their mathematics with astrology. Astrology is an ancient art that tries to blend astronomy, mathematics and the belief that the planets have powers like the ancient gods and goddesses after whom they are named. Astrologers try to use their art to interpret character and foretell the future.

Changes for the better
One of the few true mathematicians during this period, an Englishman, Roger Bacon (1214–94), tried hard to restore scientific mathematics to its former place of importance in university studies. He called mathematics the alphabet of philosophy. He had little success and eventually was accused of practising magic and was imprisoned.

Gradually ideas began to change. From the 11th century to the 13th century Christians from Europe fought a series of

SILVESTER. II. PAPA. AQVITANVS

wars in the Middle East against the Arabs. The Arabs were followers of another religion, Islam. Coming from their homelands in the Arabian deserts, these fierce warriors had found it easy to conquer the Greek-speaking world of north Africa. They pushed into Europe itself when they conquered most of Spain. They became particularly interested in Greek mathematics and science and their own scholars translated Greek works into Arabic. They produced many brilliant mathematicians of their own. They contributed a new and more efficient way of writing numbers, including the use of nought, and greatly expanded and improved algebra. Arab writings were then translated and studied in the

▲Even in the darkest period of mathematical learning, some people kept the science alive. Gerbert of Aquitaine (953–1003), who became the first French pope, Sylvester II, was a mathematician. He collected the surviving books of Latin and Greek authors to preserve their ideas. To help others do long and difficult calculations, he built globes of the earth and the heavens and popularized the use of the abacus.

►Geometric patterns, such as these marvellous ones on the Dome of the Rock in Jerusalem, where favourite decorations of the Arabs. Their religion (Islam) forbade them to make pictures of any living thing. Instead, their artists and craftsmen concentrated on abstract patterns like those in the picture. Because of the Arabs' knowledge and understanding of mathematics it is not surprising that the patterns were based on geometry. Many Muslims, as the followers of Islam are called, also believed that contemplating such perfect patterns would help them understand the perfection of God.

►The astrolabe, a mathematical instrument known to the ancient Greeks, was widely used by medieval astronomers to measure the altitude of the stars. The outer ring has the names of different heavenly bodies on it and is marked off in degrees.

European universities.

In 1453, the Turks, another people who were followers of Islam, captured the last stronghold of the old Greek-speaking world, Constantinople. Thousands of Greeks fled to Europe. As refugees they brought little with them except the knowledge of their language and sometimes a few precious books. They settled in Venice, Florence, Rome, Paris and Oxford. Wherever they went, they stirred curiosity among scholars. Slowly, out of that curiosity came the exciting adventure we now call the Renaissance. From the Renaissance were born the arts and sciences of the modern world.

GOING PLACES

The Renaissance (the word means 'rebirth') is famous for the work of some of the greatest artists the world has ever known such as Michelangelo, Leonardo da Vinci and Raphael. But it was also a time of rebirth for the sciences. Pure mathematics suddenly came to light again as a subject that excited and challenged people's minds. Not only was mathematical research encouraged by the fresh ideas coming from translations of Arab authors and the teaching of Greek refugees, but at the same time a wonderful invention made spreading information easy – the printing press. To produce many copies of a book became cheap and easy. Scientists in different countries could compare notes and share ideas quickly.

Printing also encouraged mathematicians to present their ideas in a uniform way that everyone could understand. The new Arabic numerals were accepted quickly because they were so obviously better than the clumsy old Roman ones. Long and complicated calculations became easier to do. There were other improvements in the way mathematics was written down (its notation) too. Our familiar plus, minus and equal signs ($+$, $-$, and $=$) were invented and universally accepted. Finding a square root was also given a neat sign $\sqrt{\ }$ by the German mathematician, Christoff Rudolff. It is now familiar in mathematical notation. (Finding a square root is discovering what quantity, when multiplied by itself, is equal to a given number – the square root of 9 is 3, for example.) The great mathematical works of the past, particularly Euclid's writing about geometry, were translated, printed and became generally available and well known. Algebra and trigonometry were improved with new ideas and new methods. A Frenchman, Francois Viete (1540–1603), made important contributions to both branches of mathematics. Most useful was the fact that he introduced a systematic way of using letters for both known and unknown quantities in equations. This made new and more complex operations possible.

Although applied mathematics did not appear to make so much progress as pure mathematics, in some fields its use was vital. Scientific astronomy revived. The astrological and magical cobwebs were cleared away. Nicolas Copernicus (1473–1543) was an excellent mathematician, but he was more interested in astronomy. Combining his mathematical skills and careful observation of the stars and planets he proposed that the earth moved around the sun, not the sun around the earth as people had generally believed. Later, in 1632, the Italian mathematician and astronomer Galileo supplied detailed proof of Copernicus' idea.

Mathematics aids explorers

The Renaissance also marked the beginning of the great voyages of discovery. Suddenly the maps of the world had to be redrawn. People found out, to their delight, that the great oceans were highways to new and exciting lands.

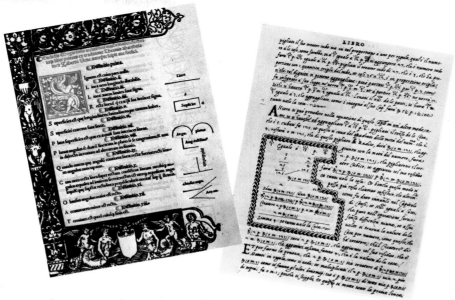

▲ The invention of printing in the 15th century helped the spread of mathematical ideas. On the left is an edition of Euclid's work. On the right is a page from a book on algebra.

▼A map of the world published in 1587 by Gerardus Mercator, the Flemish mathematician and geographer.

▲ A 16th-century compass like this one could have been used by an explorer. The disc tilts so it is always level, even when the ship rolls. The decorated arrow points North. Each small section marked off by a red line is 10°. A complete turn of the disc is 360°.

◄ Measuring time exactly is important to navigators. Before clocks were common, sailors would use an hour glass. In this 17th-century one it takes exactly one hour for the sand from the top container to fall into the bottom.

They did not mark the edges of a flat world where luckless sailors would fall off into the mouths of waiting dragons. Explorers needed mathematics to help them navigate these oceans. Navigate is a word that comes from the Latin meaning 'to sail' – we now use it to mean 'find a way from one place to another'.

For thousands of years sailors had

made long journeys out of sight of land, guided by the stars at night. For the ever longer voyages of exploration this method was not good enough. Adventurers were sailing into utterly unknown waters, to distant parts of the earth where even the stars above them would be unknown as well. The compasses they used, developed from instruments made by the Chinese and Arabs, were not very accurate. Gradually however, by using the geometry of the circle and sphere and keeping precise measurements of distance and time, navigators were able to work out their positions on the globe. The idea of exact *longitude* and *latitude* was born.

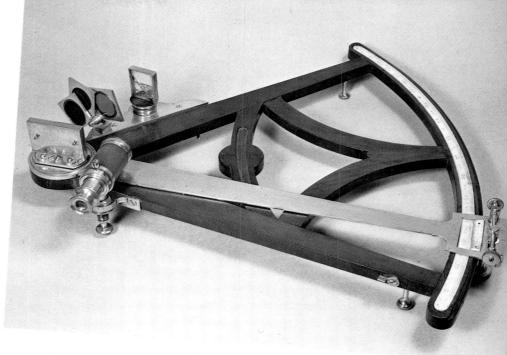

Mathematics and the arts

Mathematics also worked closely with art. The wealthy leaders of towns in Italy – Venice, Florence, Rome – wanted to build magnificent palaces, and public buildings with fine libraries. Their architects were not specialists in only designing buildings; they were artists as well, and studied mathematics to help them build beautifully proportioned buildings, and to design domed roofs for their cathedrals.

▲Sextants were used at sea to measure the height of the sun or moon above the horizon. They are more accurate than astrolabes.

◄The Piazza of the Capitol in Rome, designed by Michelangelo, one of the greatest artists working in Italy in the 15th and 16th centuries. Art and science were so closely linked that no-one thought it odd for an artist to design buildings.

3

MATHEMATICS TODAY

GREAT REVOLUTIONS

A revolution is a complete change. From the 1600s to the 1900s, there have been all sorts of revolutions. Kingdoms that had lasted a thousand years disappeared in political revolutions. The way people worked, were educated, lived and even ate changed in social and economic revolutions. One of the most important revolutions of all was that the very rate of change in our lives speeded up tremendously. Think about it. In 1600, people and books moved slowly from country to country, travelling by horse, or in a boat with sails, or often only at the speed someone could walk. Ideas made their way from university to university slowly too. Historians do not think it odd to talk about the Renaissance in Italy in 1400 and then talk about it in England or Sweden 150 years or more later. But from the 1870s to today people have been able to move faster and faster – first trains, then planes and now rockets. Information moved first by letter, then by telegraph, then by radio and now satellites link people thousands of miles apart in an instant.

Mathematics has changed enormously during this time too. In fact, it is fair to say that mathematical ideas and skills are at the heart of many of the greatest revolutions. Mathematics has provided a means to measure, plan and build the new machines that gave people totally new jobs and ways to live. It also increased its own power to investigate some of the most basic things in life: the planet on which we live, the stuff we are made of and, finally, time itself.

The mathematical revolution began in the 1600s. Before then, what was known about number, all forms of calculation, problem solving, lines and angles, flat shapes and solid forms, measurement and the ability to discover unknown quantities developed slowly. A mathematician did not expect that his own work would change his subject in any astonishing way. After the 1700s, as the work of Descartes, Pascal, Newton and Leibnitz became well known, this was no longer true. The mathematical path became a staircase. Each contribution was laid on past foundations but mathematicians understood that it was possible to push their own understanding up to a surprising new level that no one had imagined before.

René Descartes
In 1637, the French philosopher and mathematician, René Descartes (1596–1650), published a book called *Geometrie*. For the first time someone took the subject further than Euclid. Descartes corrected the Greek master on several points and applied algebra to geometry in a new *analytical* way. This means that he used new calculations to examine geometric *theorems* and the thinking behind them. His methods also made it possible to use geometry in new fields. He invented a way to study planes and curves. Most important of all, he gave mathematicians a way to do something that previously they assumed was impossible – find a point in space. Descartes also wrote brilliantly on other subjects in science and philosophy. Shortly before he died he began to study matter – that is the stuff of which everything is made, from rocks and stones to people – and motion, the way things move. These two subjects would, in this century, transform our ideas about how the world is made.

Pascal and the computer's ancestor
Blaise Pascal, another Frenchman (1623–62), made revolutionary contributions to mathematical thinking too. In 1641, when he was only 18, he invented the world's first 'arithmetic machine'. His gadget made of metal cogs and wheels could add and subtract rapidly, with perfect accuracy. Later, a German mathematician, Gottfried

◄This strange collection of rods, discs and tubes is a modern copy of the calculating machine or 'Analytical Engine' designed by Charles Babbage. Information was fed into it by punch cards, it could store data and automatically type out the result.

►This is Pascal's adding machine. The wheels have cogs and are marked from 0 to 9. As one wheel passes 9 it moves the next wheel on one place.

▼Leibnitz developed Pascal's ideas about calculating machines and built one of his own. This one dates from 1683.

Leibnitz (1646–1716), improved Pascal's machine so it could multiply and divide as well. In 1833, the idea of a machine that could do mathematical calculations inspired an Englishman, Charles Babbage. He designed one that could calculate, store the results and later accept instructions to do new calculations based on the information it 'knew'. These machines were the ancestors of the powerful modern computer.

Pascal, like Descartes, made an important contribution to geometry. His work on conic sections, the shapes that are created if you slice through a cone, was the first important development in this field of geometry since the Greek, Apollonius, who died in 200 BC! But Pascal's most important contribution grew out of letters he exchanged with another great mathematician, Pierre de Fermat (1601–65).

►'Exploded' view of a pocket calculator. The top layer, of course, has all the buttons you press, the middle one has the control circuitry and the bottom layer houses the battery.

The laws of probability

Excited by Fermat's ideas, Pascal discovered a way to express the laws of probability. These are mathematical rules that say how likely an event is to occur. An example of this would be what happens when you throw a pair of dice. If you throw them once, you would think yourself lucky to get a pair of sixes; if you throw a pair of sixes twice running you would be very lucky; if you threw the dice many more times, you would probably find that your luck petered out, and that it was a long time before another pair of sixes turned up. In fact, a pair of sixes will probably turn up only once in 6×6 throws, that is, 36 throws; if you started off with two lots of pairs of sixes you would have exhausted your chance of getting any more for at least 72 throws (two lots of 36). Probability theory does not tell us exactly when something will happen; it tells us whether something is very likely to happen or is very unlikely to happen. But the unlikely may still happen – but it may take a million years before it does!

Pascal formulated his theories and tested them by actually throwing dice and recording the patterns the numbers made.

The rules of probability are an important part of statistics, and the statistical method is one of the most widely used branches of modern mathematics. Statistics now plays a part in everything from astronomy and physics to medicine, selling toothpaste, planning TV programmes and deciding how many check-outs a supermarket needs. We use statistics to help us predict what is likely to happen, when all that we know is what happens in a general way over a longish period of time; we use what we know to try to work out what is likely to happen at a particular time – but we can never know in advance if we are right or not and whether it really will happen.

The work of Isaac Newton

Isaac Newton (1642–1727), the son of an English farmer, was one of the most creative mathematicians who ever lived. Seeing an apple fall from an apple tree made Newton wonder why it fell down and not up. Thinking about this eventually led him to discover the mathematical laws of gravity that explain how particles of matter attract – pull at – each other. Gravity is the force that keeps everything fixed to the surface of the earth and causes things to fall down and not up.

Newton not only described gravity, he also provided a mathematical way to calculate the amount of attraction that exists between objects and what sort of power or speed is needed to overcome it. Calculations of this sort are essential to many scientists, and vital to anyone who wants to design an airplane or fire a

► This diagram illustrates an experiment in probability. When you throw a pair of dice, they can stop in any of the 36 possible combinations of numbers shown. Here are the chances of making any particular score. For example, there is a much greater probability of making 7 than 2 because there is only one way you can throw a 2 but six ways you can throw a 7.

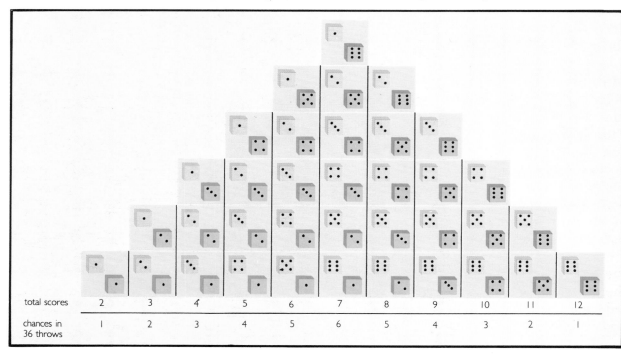

total scores	2	3	4	5	6	7	8	9	10	11	12
chances in 36 throws	1	2	3	4	5	6	5	4	3	2	1

rocket to the moon. Newton also invented mathematical techniques such as a way to solve equations where one element in the problem changes constantly. This is particularly important in physics. As he grew older, Newton spent more and more time applying mathematics to physics. Optics is the branch of physics which studies light, what it is and how it works. Newton's work reshaped that subject into its modern form.

Leibnitz and calculus

Gottfried Leibnitz is a curious but important figure in this story of mathematical change. He was as much a philosopher, politician and writer as he was a mathematician. Not only did he develop Pascal's calculating machine, he built on Newton's thought and work too. Some people say he invented integral and differential calculus. These are ways of solving complex algebraic equations. They are an essential technique of modern mathematics. Without them, much of the work of modern astronomers and physicists would be impossible. Others say that the real credit for this invention is Newton's. Certainly Leibnitz and Newton wrote many letters to each other about the calculus and Newton described many of its principles long before Leibnitz. But Newton was as shy and slow to publish his work as Leibnitz was bold and quick with his. What is absolutely certain is that Leibnitz invented the notation which integral and differential calculus use and he presented the system in a clear and usable form.

Mathematics becomes a modern science

The 18th and early 19th centuries, in Europe particularly, were an age of political revolution. At the same time, people were looking for new faiths to replace the old, just as they tried new ways of governing themselves. Science – an organized body of knowledge based on fact and tested by experiment – became for many a new kind of faith. There, at the heart of science, was mathematics. As the other sciences expanded rapidly, so did mathematics, swiftly becoming more and more complex. People soon talked

about 'higher' arithmetic, 'higher' algebra and 'higher' trigonometry. A great Swiss mathematician, Leonhard Euler (1707–83), reviewed most of the existing branches of mathematics and made important contributions to advance them all, especially geometry.

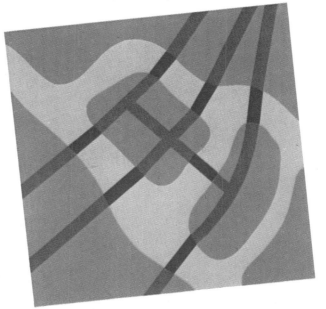

▲ Isaac Newton made many important mathematical discoveries, including the laws of gravity.

◄ Could someone walk across each of the seven bridges shown in this map and come back to the starting point without crossing any bridge twice? This was one of the earliest problems in topology. Euler proved mathematically that it could not be done.

41

Geometry developed so rapidly that soon there was a totally new variety that even Descartes would not have recognized. It began to be called non-Euclidian geometry. In 1829 a Russian mathematician, Nikolai Lobachevski, discovered a way some axioms could be rewritten to express new ideas. Later a German mathematician, August Möbius, discovered how to use mathematics to describe shapes that twisted and changed. This was the branch of mathematics later to be well known as *topology*. It was particularly concerned about what happened to patterns or networks, especially on spheres. Imagine that you drew a complicated pattern on a soft rubber ball then flattened the ball between your hands. Suppose you had to measure and describe what happened to the pattern. Topology would give you a way to do it.

As physicists plunged deeper and deeper into the secrets of matter, light and energy, mathematics became even more important to them. They were dealing with things so small, so fast or so powerful that the mind could hardly absorb the facts. Trying to test theories in practice was difficult. Mathematics gave them a way to carry on their work. It even provided practical help when they needed to build complicated machines for their experiments.

Einstein and his theory of relativity
Finally, when we come to our own time, we see the greatest mathematical revolution of all: mathematicians beginning to study the nature of time itself. Newton had done all his work assuming that space and time were just there – they always existed and always would exist and did not change in any way. Albert Einstein (1879–1955) noticed that a series of experiments in physics always gave results that no one could explain. He began to look into the problem. In 1905 he published a great piece of mathematical understanding, the theory of relativity. In it he explained that time could indeed change, go slower or faster. The rate at which it changed could affect the physical world. His theory forced all physicists to rethink the basic ideas and methods of their science.

Einstein also wrote a deceptively simple equation, $E = mc^2$. This is a quick way of saying that Energy (E) and Matter (m) are directly related; the more matter there is, the more energy can be released from it. The amount of energy is found by multiplying the amount of matter by c^2 where c represents the speed of light (or radiation), and is a constant, or unvarying, number. The speed of light is very, very fast, so that 'c' is a very big number, and c^2 is even bigger. So the equation tells us that from a very small amount of matter we can get an enormous amount of energy.

◄Albert Einstein was one of the most important mathematicians who has ever lived. Although he died in 1955, much his work still forms the basis of 'new' sciences like astrophysics.

From this equation has grown our understanding of the atom, that basic building block of the universe. As energy is represented by various forms of power, such as heat, or explosion, the equation has helped us in our efforts to get power from nuclear fuel; if we can release the enormous amount of energy inside a very small atom, we can use it to produce electricity to run our factories, and to light and heat our homes.

▼Modern science is based on such complex calculations that scientists need equally complicated machines to check that their calculations are correct. This is the Cockcroft-Walton accelerator, named after its designers, John Cockcroft and Ernest Walton. It was immensely important in the study of the atom.

MEASURING NOW

►Science is international and scientists the world over use the same systems of weights and measures. This is the standard kilo weight, kept under glass to protect it from dust and dirt. Calculations using these standard measures can be understood by scientists even if they cannot speak each other's language.

Modern systems of measurement
This is not yet true for everyday weights and measures though. Generally, three main systems are used around the world: the US customary, the British imperial and the metric. The American and British systems have units such as inches, feet, yards, ounces, pounds, pints, quarts and gallons. They are very similar but there are several differences. A gallon watertank in America holds less than a British gallon tank, for example. American cooks measure in cups, British cooks in fluid ounces. The metric system, based on tens, with sizes going up in tens, was originally worked out in France. It measures length in millimeters, centimeters, meters and kilometers, weight in grammes and kilogrammes, and volume in centiliters and liters. It is used everywhere in Europe and in many parts of Africa and Asia. Curiously enough, in America today you can hear people talking about measurements using both American and metric terms. When Britain joined the European Economic Community (the Common Market) the government wanted

▼Modern scientific measuring instruments must be as precise as the calculations for which they provide information. This is an adjustable micrometer screw. The calibrations on the right show the dimensions of the item being measured.

An Egyptian scribe could write down most of the mathematical knowledge of his time on a few sheets of papyrus and do his measuring with a cubit ruler, a piece of string and some simple scales. Today we would need hundreds of computers and several enormous libraries to hold all our mathematical knowledge. We do our measuring with all sorts of things from rays of light to *radioactive* particles. What is more important, when we measure anything scientifically, we use exactly the same units no matter where we are.

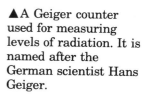

▲A Geiger counter used for measuring levels of radiation. It is named after the German scientist Hans Geiger.

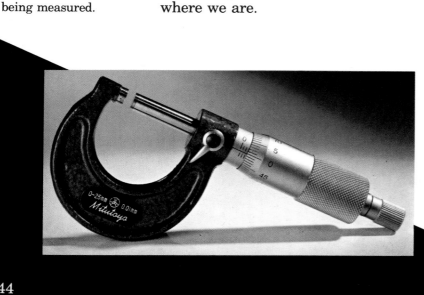

◄Theodolites are used to measure vertical and horizontal angles. They are used by surveyors and in the making of maps.

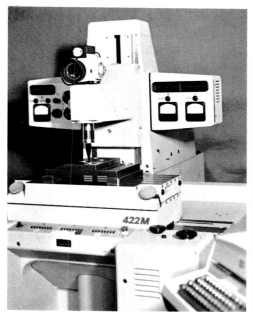

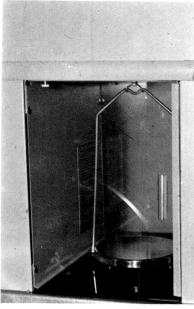

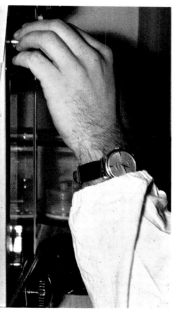

◀ Modern scientific scales are so sensitive that they are controlled from the outside of a sealed case so they are not disturbed by draughts. The weighing pan in the case is similar in shape to one used thousands of years ago but it is suspended from a delicate electronic mechanism rather than weighed against another pan. **Far left** This computer controlled machine is used to check the quality and accuracy of parts for scientific instruments.

to change the system of measurement from imperial to metric. So far, money has been changed to a decimal system. But the British are stubborn. They go on using the old names and units for many things. International trade, however, is usually done in metric measurements.

The SI system

Scientists and engineers everywhere use the SI system only, the International System of Units. This has seven basic units and includes one for mass, length, time, electricity and temperature. From these a much larger number of units are defined. It is a decimal system, that is based on ten. Smaller units are always one tenth (deci-), one hundredth (centi-), one thousandth (milli-) of the base unit. Larger units are ten times (deca-), one hundred times (hecto-), one thousand times (kilo-), the base unit. What a difference from old style scientific measures which included many odd and mysterious units such as drams, scruples and troy ounces! The range of units in the SI system makes it easy for a scientist to choose one that is suitable for the problem being studied. An astonomer does not have to measure the distance to a star in kilometers nor a biologist weigh a butterfly in kilogrammes.

Naturally the standards for each unit, that is whatever the unit is checked against, are as exact as it is humanly

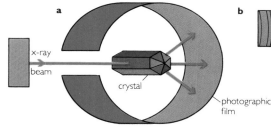

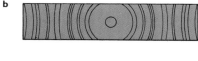

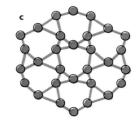

possible to make them. Because light waves are always perfectly regular and the distance between their peaks never varies, light waves provide the standard for the SI meter. And not just any light wave. The SI meter is 1,650,763.73 of a wavelength of orange light coming from the element Krypton 86. X-rays are shorter than wavelengths of visible light so they are used to measure smaller things such as layers of atoms in thin sheets of metal.

Measuring time is important too. The first really accurate clock was the marine chronometer designed for the British Longitude Board at Greenwich Observatory in 1714. The next great improvement in timekeeping was the *quartz* clock produced in America in 1929. Today the SI standard second is measured by an atomic clock that runs on a tiny particle of radioactive cesium. An atomic clock that runs for two million years will be only one minute slow at the end of that period. Since an international agreement in 1895, the base-line for all time calculations, the prime meridian,

▲ Measuring the inside of a tiny crystal is done by X-rays. An X-ray beam is shot through the crystal and when it comes out, it leaves a picture of the inside on film (**a**). The film (**b**) then is examined and the pattern of tiny dots is measured. From this pattern (**c**) the structure of the crystal can be drawn. If the crystal was unknown, the structure will identify it.

▼The red ball on the top of the Flamsteed Observatory at Greenwich, London, starts to rise to the top of the mast at 12.55 pm each afternoon. At 1.00 pm precisely the ball drops to mark the time. The white line in the cobblestones is the prime meridian. The small picture shows the 24-hour clock at Greenwich which is used as the standard for time throughout the world. has run through the Royal Greenwich Observatory, built on a hill overlooking the River Thames, just east of London. On all maps this is 0°. All navigators, at sea and in the air, calculate their position by using three pieces of information, their longitude, latitude and Greenwich Mean Time (GMT).

STATISTICS

Statistics prove 90% prefer Gleamo
Toothpaste! Statistics say 92% will vote
for Jones. Statistics show a good chance
for life in another galaxy! We all have
heard or read statements like these. They
make us suspect that statistics is just a

▼ An arrow fired at
this target has a
certain chance of
falling within each
ring. In time the hits
will build up to form a
typical 'statistical
distribution', crowded
together near the
centre, fewer farther

out. The mean, or
average, position is the
centre of the target.
The distance from the
centre inside which,
say, two-thirds of hits
fall is a measure of
their 'scatter' – the
more skilful the archer,
the less the scatter.

▼ Each point in these graphs corresponds to some value of x and y. The distance from the left side gives the value of x. The distance from the bottom is the value of y. **Below left** All points on the red line are solutions of $x + 2y = 10$. **Below right** Points on the blue line are solutions of $x - y = 1$. **Bottom** Only the values of $x = 4$ and $y = 3$ are solutions of both the equations.

Making predictions

Statisticians base their predictions on the laws of probability. There are two kinds of probability, theoretical – which is worked out purely by mathematics – and empirical, which is the result of observation and experiment. Many research problems have to use both kinds of calculation. Engineers building a new bridge for example will use calculations of theoretical probability when they check things like the safety of the design. Results of observation and experiment will give the figures for empirical probability when they are checking the strength of the metals they will use.

You may wonder why, if statistics are so mathematical and scientific, you often hear people saying that the opinion polls were wrong or the market research was a disaster. Both opinion polls and market research use statistics for their forecasts. When these fields produce poor and inaccurate statistics it usually is because the data collection was not very good. Opinion polls and market research rely on asking people questions. Planning the questions is not yet an exact science. Even a brilliant statistician will produce nonsense from poor data.

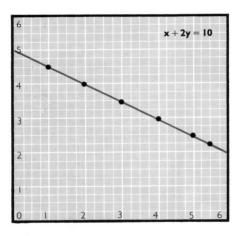

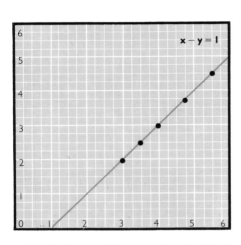

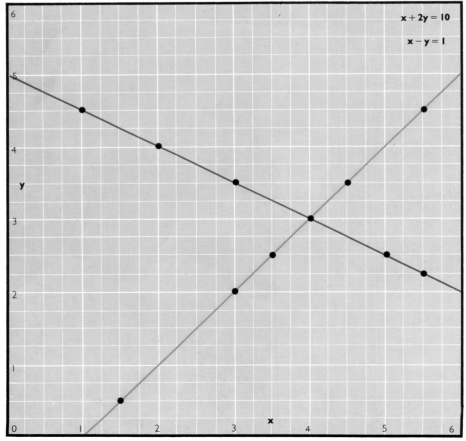

GRAPHS

We now understand there are many different ways of talking about, investigating and presenting numerical and other quantitative facts. One way which is quick and easy to understand is a graph, or special kind of diagram. The word graph is a short form of 'graphical formula'. Graphs can show complex ideas to ordinary people who perhaps would not understand how to read and make sense of many different columns of numbers. They are very good at showing how things change over a period of time. They can even give an answer to problems when there is no other mathematical way to find a solution. Most important of all, they frequently help mathematicians and other scientists to find an exact solution to problems.

Graphs are most often used to show the connection between two different things or two groups of information. If we draw a graph to show a relation between a woman's age and how much she weighs, we will, when we have finished, know more than just a set of comparisons. If we mark the bottom line of our graph with evenly spaced numbers from one to eighty and the rising line on the left hand side with weights in units of one pound or one kilo, the graph will tell us not only how quickly the woman gained weight in her early childhood and teens but how many years her weight remained level and then began to rise again or if it went up and down because of illness or diets.

Using graphs

Graphs can be used in many different ways. In algebra they are used to solve two equations which must be done at once in order to have an answer (simultaneous equations). First one equation is transferred to graph paper, then the other. The place where the lines of the two equations meet gives the answer to the problem.

Many scientific machines draw graphs, especially those used in medicine to keep a constant check on something happening in the body, like our heart beat, breathing, or the tiny little electrical signals constantly given off by our brain while we are alive. The graph made by these signals is so important that it is used to judge whether or not a seriously injured person is still alive. People who study the weather use a special kind of graph that records temperature automatically. A pen moves from side to side according to the temperature of the air and marks graph paper on a revolving drum that is turned by a clock motor.

Misusing graphs

When someone is planning to put information on a graph, he or she must be very careful to plan exactly what is to be shown and what values the intervals, the spaces, on the graph will have. If a curve is going to be drawn to connect points on a graph, its meaning too must be clearly thought out and carefully marked. If the scale and the key of the graph are not clear the information on the graph will be useless. It may even be misleading or wrong. It is easy, and quite tempting, to design a graph that makes a business look more successful, or a product more popular, than it really is – provided the key is left out.

Different types of graph

There are many different types of graph. Some just use the basic points connected by a curve. The way the curve slopes and whether or not it has just one peak will tell someone looking at it a great deal. Some graphs use simple bars or columns of colour. A pie diagram, or pie chart, is a graph that uses the circle. By showing parts of it, like slices from an unevenly

►Information about a patient's condition is obtained from sensors attached to the body. A special microprocessor interprets this data and displays the result on a special screen. This computer is designed for heart (cardiac) patients.

▲This machine is recording the patterns of the woman's brain waves. Sensors are attached to her head under the white patches. The long wavy lines on the white background show the patterns of the waves during different activities.

► Here is a way a graph can be made misleading: simply cut off half. In the top graph, the company seems to have made some sort of dramatic improvement going from £11 million to £12 million in a year. In the bottom graph we see this is less wonderful because it is really just a small increase on a very large base.

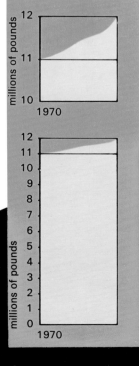

energy consumption in the USA

million million
kilowatt hours

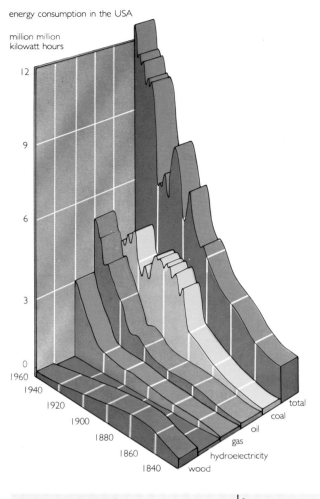

◄ Some graphs have three dimensions – length, width and height. The artist has combined this with clear colours so it is easy for us to see what sorts of power were used to make what amount of energy in which year.

► A circular pie chart is used to suggest how the world's population will be divided in the year 2000. Each circle represents the total world population for the year shown.

South America

Asia

Europe

Africa

North America

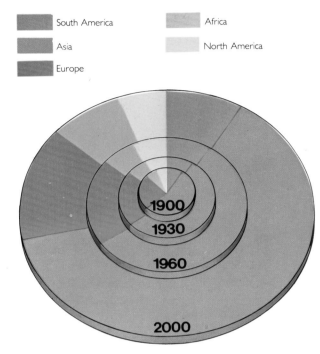

divided pie, it is easy to see what percentage of the whole is used in a particular way. It is also possible to use several circles of different sizes, one on top of the other, to show increases. Graphs are particularly helpful in making statistical reports attractive to read. Artists can often produce very clear symbols to help the reader identify each part of the graph so it is possible to cover several collections of information in one illustration.

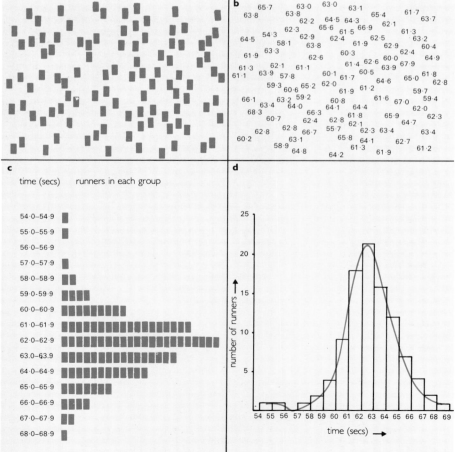

time (secs)   runners in each group

number of runners

time (secs) ➔

◄ This is the way a mass of information can be organized on to a graph. **a** shows a hundred runners of the same age group being timed over 400 m (437 yds); **b** shows the results, a disorganized group of numbers; **c** the first organization of runners into time groups. Most are in a

row that corresponds to just over 62 seconds. **d** a finished graph with each vertical bar representing the number of runners in one time group. The red smooth curve across the top of the bars compares that total performance with one of a larger group.

COMPUTERS FOR WORK AND PLAY

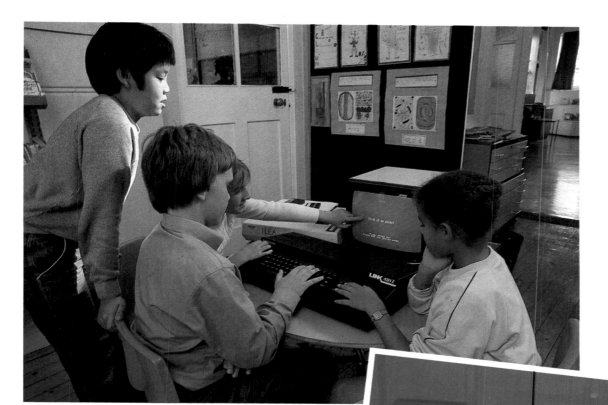

◄A computer can be an important teaching aid – it will only move on to a new problem if the first one has been solved correctly. So fast and slow learners can work at their own pace.

▼This 'floor turtle' robot is attached to a microcomputer. It can be programmed to draw different things, but was designed to teach mathematical concepts such as shapes and the relationships between different objects.

Computers are the wonder machines of modern mathematics. We are all familiar with them now. We see them – or parts of them – everywhere, at home, at school and at work. We know they have played a big part in getting men and women into space and bringing them back to earth safely. We know they can print bills and bank statements. Factories use them to control all shorts of jobs, from rolling sheet steel to painting cars. A designer of a new kind of airplane can run a check on the safety of its wings using a computer. Another kind of machine, controlled by a computer, can train a pilot to fly it. Hospitals have computers to help care for the sick. Schools and universities have computers to help run their libraries and to teach many subjects, from mathematics to foreign languages. And it is fun to relax by zapping aliens from outer space in some computer game. We can make music with a computer and draw pictures with one too.

But what are they really like and how do they work? Basically, a computer is a super-fast calculator. Unlike a calculator,

once it has been given its instructions, it does its work automatically. With a calculator, each *operation* is keyed in by the person using the machine so it can only go as fast as the person. Computers working with electric power carry out single operations in a thousand millionth of a second, a nanosecond. It is this great speed that misleads people into imagining that computers can think. Computers, even the largest and most powerful ones, cannot think. All they do is carry out, step by step, a plan of work given to them by a human being. This plan is called a program and the person who writes it is called the programmer. Once it has received its program, a computer will react to all new instructions and information fed into it by checking everything against the program to see what it must do. It can do only what it is told. It cannot invent anything new or change its program in any way.

Flow charts and languages

All computer programs begin with a Flow Chart. A flow chart looks like – and is – a kind of map. It usually is a series of boxes, each containing a single step of the operation and all connected by lines and arrows. Often the chart has loops to explain what happens if more information is needed or one path is blocked in some way. Programmers use special languages to write their instructions for computers because ordinary languages, and even ordinary mathematical notation, cannot be translated directly into a code machines can use. The easiest of these special languages is BASIC (Beginners All-purpose Symbolic Instruction Code). It is easy to learn because it seems very much like a simple kind of English. Other common computer languages are FORTRAN (Formula Translation) which is often used by scientists and mathematicians and COBOL (Common Business Oriented Language) used, as you would guess, by businessmen. In the world of computers, new words are often made from the initials of other words.

After a program is written in a computer language, it is translated into machine code using the binary number system. 'Bi-' means two and the system gets its name because it is based on two digits '1' and '0'. All the information put into a computer is coded in this way, and it makes a pattern of 0s and 1s on a magnetic tape. Any letter in the alphabet, any number or a single part of an instruction can be coded in this way. Later the information is 'read' by the machine in exactly the same way a cassette player 'reads' the music on the tape within the cassette. It passes quickly across an electronic head that picks up the millions of small electric pulses.

Computers need information

All computers, whatever their size and type, work in roughly the same way. Information is fed into the Input Unit. Sometimes this is done by using a keyboard that looks very much like an ordinary typewriter. Sometimes an

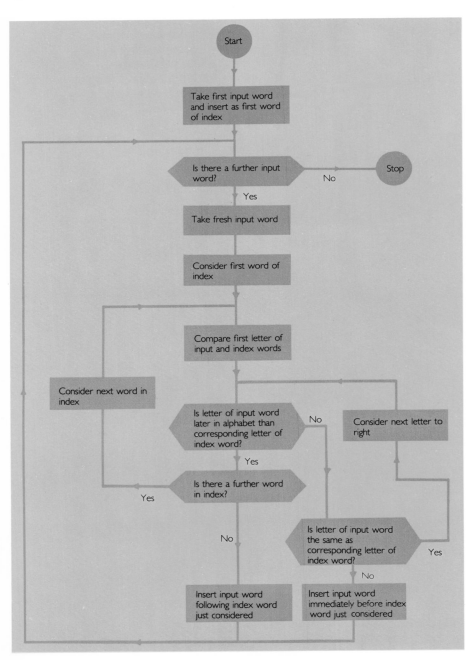

▼ A 'flow chart' of the decision-making process of a computer that has been programmed to index words alphabetically. At each stage it need merely decide 'yes' or 'no', but the final decision may depend on many simple decisions made at great speed.

operator will just drop in a spool of paper tape on which are punched millions of little holes. Some of the very large older computers 'read' their information from rectangular cards that are also covered with patterns of tiny punched holes or small markings in a special ink that can be 'read' electrically by the machine. Some of this information will become part of the computer's store, the bank of information it uses in its work or holds until needed. The rest will be the program, its working instructions. When the program is being used – or running – the instructions or calculations and transformations needed are done in a very high speed arithmetic unit. When the program is finished the results can be given in several ways. They may appear on the VDU (visual display unit) which is a small television screen. They can also come out printed on paper tape or cards. Businesses often have their results in the form of printed documents such as bills. Another common way to receive computer results is on continuous paper that folds into sheets. Usually it has been printed as the computer has worked through its program.

Sometimes the computer's 'result' is to control another machine, perhaps one that measures heat in a laboratory experiment. The computer will be connected to the other machine and may record every change of temperature on a graph. For some experiments a computer makes the perfect assistant because it never gets bored, never gets tired, never sleeps or takes a day off. And it rarely, if ever, makes a mistake.

Mainframes, minis and micros

Generally speaking, there are three types of computer: mainframe, mini and micro. Mainframes are the large and very fast computers that are used where the storage – keeping – of information is the most important part of the job to be done. You find these computers in government offices and the headquarters of large businesses where thousands and thousands of records must be kept. Minicomputers are smaller. They were first designed to help the space research program. Scientists had to be able to put

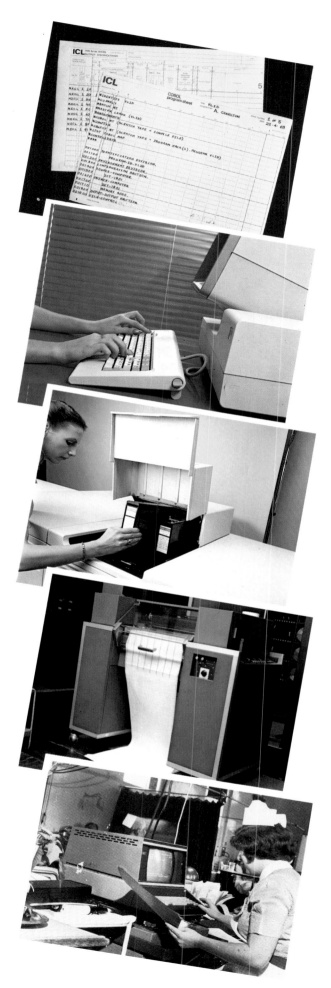

◄1 A program written in COBOL tells a computer in what order it must make each step.

◄2 An operator is keying in instructions to a computer.

◄3 Another operator is loading a computer with a discette on which information has already been coded on to large reels of magnetic tape. This is a faster way of giving a computer a memory of large amounts of data.

◄4 The computer will keep the results of a program stored in its memory but it also will print them on a continuous roll of paper so they can be read or referred to easily when the computer is doing other things. These rolls are called 'print outs'.

◄5 A nurse is using a small computer terminal with a VDU to get information about a patient from the computer's memory store.

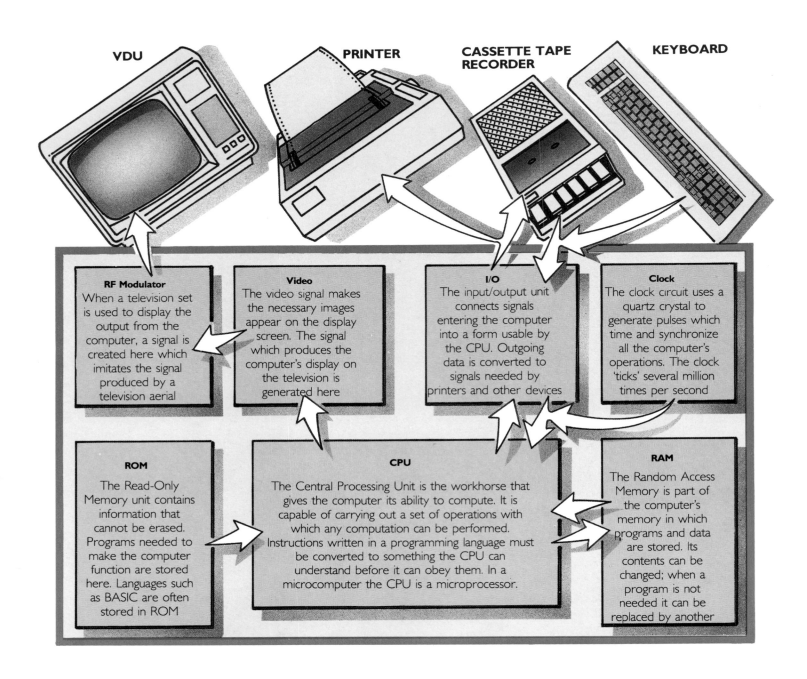

VDU

PRINTER

CASSETTE TAPE RECORDER

KEYBOARD

RF Modulator

When a television set is used to display the output from the computer, a signal is created here which imitates the signal produced by a television aerial

Video

The video signal makes the necessary images appear on the display screen. The signal which produces the computer's display on the television is generated here

I/O

The input/output unit connects signals entering the computer into a form usable by the CPU. Outgoing data is converted to signals needed by printers and other devices

Clock

The clock circuit uses a quartz crystal to generate pulses which time and synchronize all the computer's operations. The clock 'ticks' several million times per second

ROM

The Read-Only Memory unit contains information that cannot be erased. Programs needed to make the computer function are stored here. Languages such as BASIC are often stored in ROM

CPU

The Central Processing Unit is the workhorse that gives the computer its ability to compute. It is capable of carrying out a set of operations with which any computation can be performed. Instructions written in a programming language must be converted to something the CPU can understand before it can obey them. In a microcomputer the CPU is a microprocessor.

RAM

The Random Access Memory is part of the computer's memory in which programs and data are stored. Its contents can be changed; when a program is not needed it can be replaced by another

▲Several units must be connected together to form a computer system. This simplified diagram shows the units at the top and what happens in each part is described in the boxes. The arrows show which parts link up with each other.

in information from several sources fast and carry out complex equations quickly. Microcomputers are the ones we see most often in our homes and schools. Their input and output units are keyboards and VDUs. Their programs and memories are usually housed in neat cassettes. Even smaller microcomputers with fixed – that is unchangeable – programs are built into things like dish washing machines, kitchen scales and even watches. This is possible today because the thousands of electrical circuits needed in such programs can be printed on to silicone chips – minute pieces of silicone.

'Talking' computers

Although computers cannot think, they can communicate with each other and other machines. One computer can be linked to another electronically. They can, if they are programmed to do so, exchange information. It is also possible for computers to be linked to the telephone system. Then people can gain access – that is use the information in them – by telephone. Coding information for computers is so advanced now that some computers can begin work on a spoken command. The machine has not really learned to understand speech.

What happens is that the sound pattern of a word is broken into individual bits, almost like notes of music. Then each 'note' can be coded into the binary system. That pattern then triggers the right electrical pulses to start a program running or carry out some special part of a program.

Some computers are able to produce their results in a kind of speech. They do this by picking out of their memory store the coded bits that make tiny fragments of sound. They then connect these together in a way that matches a sound pattern they have been given. These sounds are played together very rapidly and we hear the computer 'speak' a word. A simpler way for a computer to 'speak' is for it to play back, on command of its program, selections from pre-recorded tapes.

Competing against computers

When you play a game with a computer, you really are playing against the mind of the person who designed the program and created the information store containing the rules of the game. The program tells the computer what moves are possible. It also gives the computer a general instruction sometimes known as the 'minimax rule'. This rule tells the computer it must always make all moves with minimum risk to its own position and to gain the maximum amount of points. Using the information in its store and its program, the computer responds to your moves. It seems so clever just because it is so fast.

'Dangerous' machines

You may wonder why, if computers can do so many useful and even entertaining things, some people talk as if they were dangerous. In science fiction stories it is not unusual for a computer to be the 'bad guy'. Probably the most famous evil computer of all was the one that went mad in the movie *2001* and almost succeeded in killing all the astronauts. A real computer cannot go 'mad' because it

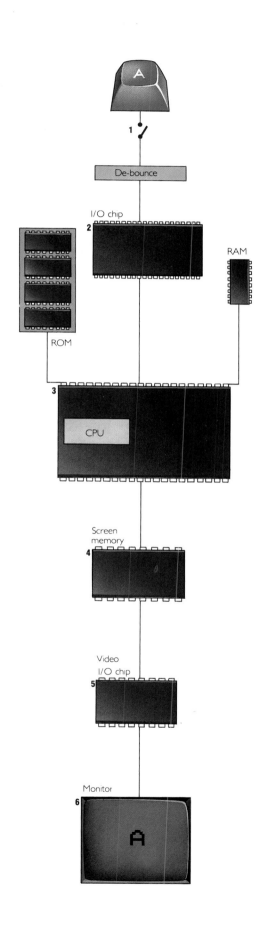

◀ The usual result of pressing a key on the keyboard is that the character represented by that key appears on the screen. When the CPU is expecting a key to be pressed, it tells the I/O Controller to 'poll' the keyboard (examine every key to see if one is being pressed) constantly. When it discovers that a key *has* been pressed, it passes the code of that key (a number less than 256) back to the CPU, which stores it as a *variable* (the name given to a single piece of information). The CPU then stores the newly-entered character in RAM (temporary memory) together with the rest of the information which will appear on the screen with it. The code is stored in two places because it is not only the CPU that has access to the special part of RAM called the Screen Memory. The Video Controller also looks through this memory, many times per second, to make sure that the character shown on the screen is the one that should be there. The character itself is not stored. Instead, the Video Controller gets from ROM the image of the character that is represented by the code, and then shows the 'picture' of that character on the screen. The images are refreshed (that means they are re-displayed) 25 or 30 times per second, because a TV screen cannot retain an image any longer than that. The De-Bounce switch ensures that a character is not accidentally repeated.

▲ Computers are becoming increasingly good at playing games. Whether you want to be a famous explorer or defeat a chess expert, the computer will help you fulfil your dream.

▼ The ultra-fast processing power and enormous storage capacity of modern computers means that it is possible to make an image on film or the television screen that is indistinguishable from a real photograph.

has no brain to go mad with. People also sometimes say that soon computers will be so powerful they will run everything and there will be no place for human beings. Since all computers must have programs and only human beings can write programs, this is not so. Computers will, however, take over many of the boring jobs that people have always hated doing.

The GIGO gremlin

Two other complaints about computers are that they often make terrible mistakes and take idiotic decisions. These criticisms certainly are not fair to computers. True, an electrical fault or a broken part can make them produce weird results but these things are quickly spotted and corrected. In the early days of big computers, in the 1950s and 1960s, computers were much more delicate and more inclined to break down than they are today. Our modern computers are remarkably tough and trouble free. As for the so-called 'decision-making' computers, they 'decide' only on the basis of what their programs and information stores tell them. They can sift through

▲This is the Jet Propulsion Laboratory, Pasadena, California, during the Voyager I Saturn mission in 1981. The computers interpret the digital information sent back by the satellite. There are three views of Saturn's rings: two on the big screens and one on the small screen on the left.

►Large computers such as this one are known as mainframes to distinguish them from mini- and microcomputers. They need a team of highly trained operators and can run hundreds of programs at the same time, sending the results all over the world by satellites, telephone lines and microwave links.

thousands of alternatives faster than we can, but it is us who must give them their material. When a computer produces some useless result, programmers and operators often laugh and say 'GIGO is operating'. GIGO is one of the oldest words in the new language of computers. It means 'Garbage In, Garbage Out'. In other words, the computer is only as good as the instructions it has received from its human master.

LEARNING THE PROCESS

Now that we live in a world of statistics, computers and pocket calculators, can we guess where mathematics will take us in the future? Obviously computers will become more and more important. They are sure to become even smaller, more simple to use and more powerful. This means that many people must learn the clear thinking skills that are needed to write programs. This will make the best use of the powers computers give us to do so many things fast and well. Learning basic mathematical processes will become more and more important. We will all need to understand how we can move from one idea to another through a chain of connected operations.

The teaching of mathematics in schools all around the world is changing quickly so that children can have the chance to learn this skill. Most people now accept that mathematics is not just a subject for a few clever children but something everyone needs to learn. The new ways of teaching mathematics make sure children understand what they are doing. They even show both children and adults that mathematics can be fun, too. In the new maths classrooms calculators and computers are part of the furniture. Like the blackboards and chalk of the past, they have become ordinary tools to help us think and work.

New uses for computers

In the business world we know computers are used to store huge quantities of information cheaply and easily. They also carry out many jobs that used to be done by poorly paid clerks, things like keeping payroll records and tax returns. Now, as mathematicians expand the regions of higher mathematics, business computers can also be used to work out problems in modelling theory. Modelling theory is a branch of mathematics in which calculations are used to give people a very accurate idea of what happens if they take a certain course of action. For example, a big international business can use a program based on modelling theory to see what would happen if it opened three new offices in different countries,

changed the prices of some of the things it made or put aside a large sum of money for research.

Governments are using modelling theory more and more now. It helps them make decisions about taxes, public works and financial planning. Armies and navies use modelling theory when they play war games – imagining what would happen to them under different kinds of enemy attack. Mathematics gives anyone who has to make important decisions in any field a very clear way of setting out the problem. This helps a person to be sure that he or she has not missed out some important factor that could change the whole result.

An increasingly important subject

In all the sciences, mathematics is gradually playing a greater and greater part. The whole purpose of scientific investigation is to study things with great exactness. Using computers even in sciences like biology – the study of living things – means that thinking must be very precise. Remember a computer program is really just a very long string of simple questions that must be answered yes or no.

It is easy to guess that the most exciting mathematical research of the future will centre around our attempts to conquer space and control atomic energy. Every part of space exploration depends on precise measurement and judgement. To navigate through space where our ordinary ideas of up and down, north and south, no longer apply is the greatest problem in three-dimensional geometry that can be imagined. To understand the blasts of enormous power and energy that fly out of the heart of an atom when it is split is something that can only be explained mathematically.

A science for everybody

One of the lovely things about all the new challenges and the different ways that mathematics can go is that it is all connected. A mathematician working out a series of very difficult equations in a university laboratory is using many of the same skills a small child uses when learning to measure water or sort things into sets and see how they relate to each other. Learning to see relationships between numbers, patterns, equations, shapes and quantities is the basic exciting mathematical adventure that can be enjoyed at any age and at any level of skill. Indeed, throughout the history of mathematics, many of its greatest geniuses began their creative work when they were teenagers.

When he was living in Princeton, New Jersey, the great mathematician Albert Einstein sometimes helped a neighbour's small child with her mathematics homework. When he was asked by another professor if he really could be bothered to do something so simple, Einstein replied, 'Yes, and I think over the years I probably have learned more from her than she learned from me.'

▲A classroom like this must be every computer maker's dream! But it is a sign of the increasingly important part that computers are playing in education. This, in turn, will have an effect on other aspects of our lives. But computers are not yet a solution to every problem. The idea of shopping from an armchair, choosing things with your home computer may seem nice, but what happens if you want to try something before buying it?

GLOSSARY

Algebra/algebraic The branch of mathematics that uses symbols to represent numbers and unknown things.
Analytic/analytical Something that is studied in great detail by looking carefully at all its parts.
Astronomer Someone who studies the stars scientifically.
Atom The smallest unit of matter.
Axiom A self-evident truth, such as: the sun always rises in the east.
Calculator display The space on the face of a calculator where the steps of the calculation are shown as they are entered and where the answer appears.
Chemistry/chemist The science that studies what substances are made of and how they change when combined with each other.
Correlate Joining two ideas or two groups of calculations or batches of information to discover if there is a relationship between them.
Digit Any number from 1 to 9.
Estimate To make a sensible guess, based on knowledge, reasoning and experience, of what the answer to a problem will be.
Galaxy A huge family of stars (and their planets).

▼The Whirlpool Galaxy, is shaped in a spiral, like our own galaxy. Without mathematics, space exploration and the discovery of distant galaxies would be quite impossible.

▼Gerardus Mercator with his globe of the world.

Geometry The mathematical study of the relationships between lines, points, angles, surfaces and solids.
Hypotenuse The side opposite the right angle in a right angled triangle.
Integer A whole number.
Latitude An imaginary line running east—west around the earth at regular intervals north or south of a central line called the equator.
Longitude An imaginary line around the earth running from north to south measured in degrees starting with the meridian, 0° longitude, which passes through Greenwich, England.
Matter The basic stuff everything in the universe is made of.
Molecules A group of atoms joined together.
Number pattern An orderly arrangement of numbers that repeats itself.
Operation A single step or task in a calculation or computer program.
Philosopher Someone who studies or teaches a system of basic principles, especially those that try to explain how we can become wise or understand how the universe works.
Physics/physicist The science that studies matter and energy.

Plane A flat surface.

Pyramid A solid figure whose base is a square and each of its four sides a matching triangle.

Quartz A hard glassy substance, usually colourless.

Radioactive Giving off tiny bursts of atomic particles.

Science Knowledge gained by carefully examining things and testing all theories against facts.

Set theory The mathematical ideas that help us sort objects and see how they are related to each other.

Statistics The collection and study of numerical information.

Symbol A sign, word or object that stands in for an idea, number or operation and represents it.

Symmetry The quality of perfect balance, when the right side is a reflection of the left.

System An orderly plan.

Tables Lists of numerical information, set out in an orderly way so that the information is easy to understand.

Theorem A statement that can be proved logically if certain axioms are accepted at the beginning of the proof.

Theory An organized explanation about what something is or why something happens. In science, it is usually based on observation and testing but it can just be the result of careful thinking about a problem.

Topology The geometry of curved surfaces.

Unit A single fixed quantity.

University A place where men and women come together to study the arts and sciences at a high level. A college is a group of teachers and students within a university.

▼ A 16th-century scholar at work, making calculations with a pair of compasses. What a contrast this room is, with its four-poster bed, fireplace and dog, to modern laboratories where the instruments are so delicate they must be protected from dust and draughts!

INDEX

Acknowledgments

Bibliotheque Nationale,
Paul Brierley, Camera
Press, Crown Copyright,
Daily Telegraph Colour
Library, Ian Dobbie,
Martin Dohrn, Mary
Evans Picture Library,
Henry Grant, Graphion,
Haags Gemetzmuseum,
Historical Picture
Service, Michael
Holford, IBM, ICL,
Archivio IGDA,
International
Computers Ltd, Mansell
Collection, Ian
McKinnel, Optimus
Cambridge,
Picturepoint,
Popperfoto, Prestel Ltd,
Scala, Science Museum
London, Science Photo
Library, Ronald
Sheridan Photo Library,
Spectrum Colour
Library, John Wallace,
Wolfenbuttel/Herzog
August Bibliothek,
Diana Wyllie, ZEFA.